FAST FOOD FOR THE SOUL

12/12/09

Donald Charles Lacy

FAST FOOD FOR THE SOUL

Nourishing Inspiration in Today's Hectic World

Donald Charles Lacy

Providence House Publishers
PROVIDENCE PUBLISHING CORPORATION
FRANKLIN, TENNESSEE

Printed in the United States of America

09   08   07   06   05   1   2   3   4   5

Library of Congress Control Number: 2005928829

ISBN: 1-57736-351-5

Cover design by Joey McNair

PROVIDENCE HOUSE PUBLISHERS
an imprint of
Providence Publishing Corporation
238 Seaboard Lane • Franklin, Tennessee 37067
www.providence-publishing.com
800-321-5692

Dedicated in gratitude
to the
state of Indiana
where I
was born,
educated,
taught school,
served churches,
reared a family,
promoted Christian unity,
and wrote prolifically

Foreword

In a hectic world where there never seems to be enough time, Dr. Donald Charles Lacy offers fast food for the soul through this interesting collection of newspaper columns.

He's written these short vignettes for the *Courier-Times*, a daily newspaper in New Castle, Indiana, over the past seven years. The pieces don't take long to read but often stick with you like grandmother's cooking—nutritional morsels of spiritual truth presented in a non-denominational way.

From advice about dealing with the death of a loved one to commentary on politics and many more topics, Dr. Lacy's writing is timely but not time-consuming. It requires no great effort or reference material to understand, but may inspire the reader to turn to the Holy Bible for more reading on a particular topic.

While there is often some gentle preaching going on in his text, Dr. Lacy's writing style is more apt to make the readers feel they've met him in a coffee shop than listened to him from the pews of a church. The beauty of this collection is that it can be taken anywhere the reader may be going and fit in any schedule. It is truly "inspiration to go," drawn from the wellspring of Dr. Lacy's forty-plus years in the ministry and created in a spirit of Christian love. It's truly fast food for the soul that's always fresh, always warm, and has no expiration date.

—Darrel Radford, managing editor
Courier-Times
New Castle, Indiana

Preface

The columns, now three-hundred or so, have been truly a labor of love. They were written for the people of east central Indiana, especially those in Henry County. My own entrance into this life began in Stoney Creek Township, near the town of Blountsville. I have never forgotten my roots and the good people who helped me mature from a skinny little timid boy to a man who spent virtually his entire adult life in the ordained ministry of the United Methodist Church. The Blountsville Elementary School, which no longer exists, was the formal beginning of my education. Teachers Marie Buell and June Stanley were key influences in my early formation. I might add my parents, Charles and Marian (Walradth) Lacy were caring and loving. Grandparents, Guy and Christie (McCall) Lacy and Glade and Grace (Gibson) Walradth were very special people. A note of thanks to the *Courier-Times* and Darrel Radford for allowing me the opportunity to write a few words each week to aid precious persons in the pilgrimage of life. Sandy Moore was also kind and considerate, as she perused each column. While reading this collection of ninety-nine, which is a carefully selected sampling, give thanks to the Living God for His blessings.

—Donald Charles Lacy

"**H**e (she) makes me so mad!" I guess that is a universal feeling from time to time among all of us. Why do you suppose this is such a common experience? There are probably many answers to my question. There is, however, one that continually sticks out in my mind.

Someone has said or done something that really rattles us. An explosion of some sort goes on inside us. I am not speaking of a momentary irritant that can be caused by not feeling well. This is an emotion that plants its feet.

To press the matter further, we discover the rattling keeps right on rattling. Only temporary relief comes. Somehow we just can't let loose of it.

If you are like I am, an inventory of self begins to take place. "Why can't I let loose of that bad feeling? It's beginning to make me ill and uncomfortable."

Well, of course, you can't go around all day meditating on your belly button. But you can take moments of time to inquire of the Creator what this is all about. Helpful? Yes.

My experience is that sooner or later, ongoing anger involves "a soul that is downcast." In short, there is depression. Life about other matters is also not going well.

Having figured that out, my understanding of life generally comes into focus. There are some things that need to be straightened out. My anger is related to other matters.

What are the other matters? Wow, that takes honesty and humility, doesn't it? There is a big grudge lodged in my past and it just doesn't seem to want to budge.

Sometimes we can move the furniture around in a house and it doesn't change anything. We thought it would, but it didn't. Maybe we need a surgeon's scalpel.

It is a lifelong process, isn't it? Our internal selves can be mini–civil wars. Yet, think how helpful it is to know getting mad and staying mad does have an answer.

To be sure, to know what causes a strongly negative feeling is not to destroy it. At the same time, we now have a handle. Socrates said, "Know thyself." That's Course 101 in life.

"What's a green-eyed monster?" If you are a parent, what is your answer? I suppose most of us would give something like this: "It's being jealous of what someone else has."

Who hasn't felt the pangs of envy? Even in the story of the prodigal son, we discover the elder brother has a problem. Why let some "dumb-dumb" be restored to the family?

When we pursue that story a little further, some of us get a glimpse of ourselves that is painful. If you are going to be forgiven anyway, why be good? It's an age-old inquiry.

Every person I have ever known has envious feelings. It helps to ask, "Why am I like that?" and to ponder our answers in solitude.

"You are good-looking and well-dressed. I hate you!" We chuckle at such openness, but it tells something deeply embedded. Is it even possible to change this human trait?

One answer I have found helpful is to be reminded of something. What is that something? Well, I call it the compensating factor that gives perspective. Don't we always have something the other guy doesn't? I think so. In fact, I think everyone produces jealousy in another person one way or another.

Note the common problem we all face. Even noble and religious people are drawn into such scrapes. For example, how would you feel if you heard that your old roommate had become a bishop?

Does any good come out of envious feelings? I think so. The green-eyed monster is like most other monsters; it must be tamed.

We tame it by recognizing it and dealing with it. Everyone of us has the potential to do this. Not to recognize and deal with it is disastrous.

Helpfulness begins with honest recognition, doesn't it? Hiding from one's real self just doesn't get it. To attempt to live life with adoring mirrors that don't show the truth is denial.

Well, where else does all of this take us? Hopefully into an internal land that has external positive effects. We are all dependent on such therapy.

I love internal and external tranquility, don't you? It is possible. We are blessed by common sense and the drive to live peaceably in a conflict-ridden society.

Taking a Close Look at Lust and Its Consequences

"**I** am in lust, not in love," a young lady said to me the other day. It is worth pondering and, in fact, deserves high marks for open honesty. However, physical attraction is not the real thing.

I have heard reputable people say, "Think about having sex with anyone you want. Just don't act on your thoughts."

Is that okay? It seems to me we had better look again.

Do thoughts translate into actions? Well, we know the answer to that one. Virtually everything we do at some point has been in our thought processes.

So, lust is a phenomenon and at the same time a powerful reality. It is one thing for an elderly person to righteously condemn lust and sexual transgression. It is quite another to admit, "I was young once, too." Our lives are in stages.

Perhaps nothing is so hurtful as sexual misbehavior. Something that seems right and natural can have terribly significant consequences. Trust and respect seem to slip away.

Lust needs to be recognized and confronted as something deeply human. It is universal. In the right circumstances husbands and wives find true bliss.

Is there a lot of difference in the way generations handle lust? I think so. Opportunity to express one's lustful urges seems far more prevalent in the last fifty years.

How about our parents and grandparents? I knew all four of my grandparents very well. They were all hard workers who found there wasn't much time for sexual escapades.

In my own lifetime, which now spans three generations, I believe one thing in particular has changed. Right and wrong have become irrelevant. Why is that?

An age-old verity is that life simply cannot be lived abundantly without self-discipline.

Can we relearn this in a realm fraught with serious problems? We must.

A very serious lady said to me, "Isn't it terrible children have to be raised by grandparents today."

Well, I don't know. My grandparents spoiled me and I loved it.

As I reflected, my mind and heart took a short trip. I drove out of New Castle on Brown Road and found my way to the Mooreland Cemetery. As usual, it was well kept.

There, I quickly found the tombstone of my maternal grandparents. They were Glade and Grace Gibson Walradth. I shed a tear or two and began to remember some great times.

He was a livestock dealer and farmer. Often, as a boy, he would take me to the sale barns; some days I can still hear the auctioneers. Boy, was that fun.

She always had a sacrificial way about her that I have never forgotten. She was a woman who did hard physical work but was also cultured, quoting poetry. She was such a caring lady.

Then my mind and heart went on up the road to the Blountsville Cemetery. There, like a little rock of Gibraltar, I spotted another tombstone. Yes, there was another tear or two.

This was where my paternal grandparents were laid to rest. They were Guy and Christie McCall Lacy. They were such precious hardworking and strong people.

He was a plasterer and applied his trade across east central Indiana. He took his grandson at the ripe old age of fourteen and told him it was time to carry the hod. He was a kind man.

She made the best prune cakes and always saved things for me. She used to kid her grandson about his girl friends, even before he had one. She was special and never flashy.

Indeed, it is a different day and time for many across our land. Family brokenness is obvious.

What's happened to us? Why is it necessary for many today to raise both their children and grandchildren? Those questions have bothered me for years and they still do.

There's always enough blame to go around for everyone. So, why not appreciate who and what we can? I was very privileged and shall forever be grateful, even sentimental.

Humanity sooner or later passes through times and obligatio
that just don't seem right. Remember, every potential tragedy is also
a potential triumph. Hooray for grandparents.

5 Faith Can Carry Us Through the Most Difficult Situations

During a quiet moment at the funeral home, he said, "She was a woman of great faith." He was her surviving husband who loved her deeply. Yet, it was her faith he cherished.

She had given birth to eight children, only six were still living and two of them had died tragic deaths. One was killed in a speeding automobile and the other was murdered.

Sometimes her husband wasn't much help and he knew it. Yes, he spent too much time in the bars and he knew it. He was even known to hit her once in awhile.

When she worked at a local grocery to help make ends meet, he was not much help. She could get there and back by whatever means she could find. He didn't need her money.

Near the end of her life, he seemed finally to grow up. In fact, for him to admit she was a woman of great faith produced as much anger as compassion.

After all, virtually everyone who knew the family could testify to her faith. She just never gave up on her children and her husband. Most were in awe.

When every deck was stacked against her, she persisted. God, she believed, had given her eight children and her husband. There would be no giving up.

How about you and me? Is staying the course in life sometimes not only painful but virtually impossible? Do we have the faith to succeed eventually?

For countless numbers today, staying together as a family is a test of faithful endurance. Yet, how else do we preserve basic principles? Only a sturdy faith can see us through.

I have often marveled at the number of wives and mothers whose faith simply would not be defeated. There are untold numbers who provide glue to hold us together. Praise God.

idn't her husband come to his senses sooner? We all have
swers to that. Frankly, I believe fathers must grow sons
⌐y big faith. When fathers fail sons, their sons' wives and
…eir children are at a high risk. So much depends on the father-son
relationship. Producing men of great faith begins at birth.

A saint said long ago, "Husbands, love your wives just as Christ
loved the church and gave his life for it." What we firmly believe sets
our priorities. Faith can carry the day.

6   Take Time to Know Our Teachers

"**T**here aren't any good teachers anymore," said Mr. Crabby of
Complainsville, U.S.A. That's about the most preposterous
thing I have heard in a long time. Of course, there are good
teachers today.

My first recollection of a teacher was Mrs. Marie Buell in the
first grade at Blountsville. Would you believe she always prayed
before we ate at noon? I can't recall the words, only the respect.

Many years later it dawned on me what she gave me in the class-
room. She was the epitome of stability and security. We were in safe
hands and she was a permanent fixture.

Are there women and men much like her today in the early years
of school? Yes. Yes. Yes! I'll also bet there is a lot more prayer done
in those classrooms than some suspect.

I must confess my favorite teacher was a relative. Her name was
Aunt Marjorie Lacy Luellen. Her husband, a former trustee of
Stoney Creek Township, died quite unexpectedly.

What did she do? Well, she started college and eventually earned
a graduate degree. She used to laugh about getting all done before
she had to retire to a rocking chair.

Marjorie was a sweet and very intelligent woman. She was a
pillar in the Blountsville Christian Church and a former postmaster.
And she was a Democrat, and I mean a Democrat.

Her teaching career lasted twenty-two years, all in the Union
School Corporation of Randolph County. She especially distin-
guished herself as a sponsor of Little Hoosiers. Bless her heart.

A log house literally was brought to the school in her memory and restored. You think there aren't any good teachers anymore? Well, she taught all of her years after 1970.

I always wanted to see her have a doctorate degree but that didn't happen. Some of us tried but couldn't get that done. But it doesn't matter because St. Peter probably calls her "Doc" in heaven.

You see, flesh and blood, dedicated to education in the broadest sense makes for good teachers. They are all around us. We do have to take the time to know them.

Take your child's teachers aside and tell him or her you appreciate their work. Isn't teaching a ministry? It is, and there are no easy positions in the school systems today.

I loved the three years I taught history and English in Jay County. Maybe it was because I had a really good grounding in practice teaching. That was done in the old New Castle High School.

7   Is Comfort at Any Price Worth It?

"Comfort is necessary and I won't do without it," someone said in a deeply serious manner. At the time this statement conveyed nothing out of the ordinary. But then, is this healthy?

I suppose we all have the need to be comfortable in most circumstances. But does that assume comfort at any price? Are we prepared to do whatever is necessary . . . just in case?

We have begun with an apparently innocent and natural feeling. I am not so sure that is altogether healthy. Maybe we could do without an air conditioner a day or two, maybe three.

Please accept an invitation to play the game of "what if." I think you will find it helpful and a bit frightening. Remember we are playing a game with real consequences.

What if a group of terrorists is able to capture key military points in our country? What if they are able to penetrate our banking system? What if there is betrayal by our own?

What if these dangerous gangsters infiltrate the media centers? What if they succeed in kidnapping key governmental and business leaders? What if they bring us to our knees?

Under those conditions, the insistence on comfort offers a demonic opportunity. Their game plan becomes obvious. Begin to imagine the offer we are going to receive.

Such sinister folks tell us not to put up a fight. In other words, go on watching TV and eating your favorite dishes. We will guarantee you comfort, but we are taking over.

We are promised very little bloodshed. Few—if any—paychecks will be missed. We are not to resist and all will go well with us and our intense desire to be comfortable.

Of course, the problem becomes that it is no longer really our country. We have preferred a life of relative ease to the anguish of battle. Our patriotism is at a low ebb.

I don't know about you but that just scares the dickens out of me. The whole scenario makes one hurt. It tells me the Stars and Stripes are expendable.

I want to shout, "Dear Lord, how did this happen to the home of the free and the brave?" I want to say this isn't even good material for a novel. Yet, I ponder the possibility.

Please ponder all of this on your knees. Then sing at the top of your voices, "God Bless America." Then decide, if need be, that comfort is not necessary and you can do without it.

8   Prayer is Powerful, Even in Mixed Crowds

"Prayer is the most powerful force in the world." This statement comes to us from many, Christian and even non-Christian. Most of us know the truth it sends. Prayer is powerful stuff.

My travels have taken me into a variety of religions over the years. Can Jews and Christians pray together? Well, yes, because I have been there when it happened and it is marvelous.

Can Baptists, Methodists, Presbyterians, Lutherans, Nazarenes, and Catholics pray together? Of course, we do it all the time. If we aren't able to, the Master's call to be one is muted.

Perhaps the most unique moment of prayer I have experienced was at a gathering of Scottish Rite Masons and the Knights of

Columbus in South Bend. Can such apparently different groups come together and pray? You bet they can.

For some years these men have been meeting together in the spring for a series of talks. I was their speaker one year and couldn't tell the difference between Protestants and Catholics. That's the truth.

Did we have prayer together? Unquestionably, the answer is yes, and we couldn't find the labels on our foreheads to differentiate us. Surprisingly, we didn't seem to experience discomfort.

Prayer builds bridges over chasms we once thought impossible. Prayer can put men together in places some would say is beyond possibility. Prayer is the key to Christian unity.

What can explain the great and sudden power of the Promise Keepers? Prayer. All at once, this movement exploded to inspire and heal bewildered men.

Prayer warriors were busy at work long before the movement seemed to come out of nowhere. Men and women were on their knees in ways we had not seen for some time.

While it is beyond my knowledge, I suspect there were as many wives and mothers praying as there were husbands and fathers. Promise Keepers was given birth and guided by prayer.

Our subject is unlimited. The thousands of books that have been written on prayer do not exhaust its meaning. In a sense, every time a new baby is born new prayer-life is born.

Our personal prayer lives always need to be addressed. Go without praying for a few days and see what happens. Our spiritual strength sags and moves toward depletion.

Sometimes, dear friends, that best thing we can do on our knees is to say, "Here I am Lord. Please help me." Then be quiet until the Lord speaks . . . and He will.

Music Speaks to Everyone

I have often pondered the saying, "Music is the only universal language."

It intrigues me because there is an abiding truth in the statement. Music speaks like nothing else.

Even though I am not a musician, it has spoken to me uniquely above virtually everything. The only exception would be the Holy Bible. Then, I enjoy the lyrical quality of the Psalms.

It seems there is nothing on the face of this earth that moves so many people. Those of us who are dunces in this field, nevertheless, immerse our heads and hearts. What a gift from God.

Music has motivated men for centuries to battle bravely for their nations. In our nation, soldiers, sailors, and marines have sung the national anthem while determined to give their lives if necessary.

History books tell us of the superhuman bravery of the soldiers who surrounded Napoleon Bonaparte. His charisma was supported by music. With an emotional splendor, they died for him.

Brahms, Beethoven, Mozart, and Bach all conjure up feasts of emotional, mental, and spiritual involvement. Such genius takes us into pure ecstasy. Heaven is near.

Gospel music with such gifted people as Bill and Gloria Gaither can cause torrents of tears. Our feelings receive an injection of love. Try to count the smiles.

The whole field is so enormous we prove and discover only a smattering of what has been given to us. Who is to say what is better than another? Highbrow or lowbrow—who cares?

Take country music. Try to name all of the performers and you can get a very large headache. Willie Nelson, Dolly Parton, and Garth Brooks are only a beginning.

I am reminded of my grandfather, Guy Lacy, who never made it into high school. That didn't matter. He had his own musical tastes and his oldest grandson loved them.

One hot summer day, my grandfather and I were sent to the old Princess theater in New Castle on a work detail. We were to patch the outside walls. We were a good team.

On a late afternoon, I heard singing and clapping inside the Princess. Grandfather had disappeared. Finally I found him at the rear of the building with his ear to the wall.

Little Jimmy Dickens was on stage belting out "Take an Old Cold Tater and Wait" and "May the Bird of Paradise Fly Up Your Nose." The dear man had an angelic smile. Don't argue with that.

10   When Confronted with Change, Consult Your Inner Self

As a husband and wife were moving into another home, the wife was overheard to say, "I just hate change." She was serious, even though the new one was better. Sounds like you and me.

We get used to an environment and are reasonably happy in it, so we avoid change like the plague. Is this a good way to live one's life? In today's world, the answer is "yes and no."

Not to be ready and willing to change in today's world is probably to admit failure. Moving here and there today has become commonplace. We do it to survive.

At the same time, one of the most positive things I see in our society is that many people in the work force refuse to move strictly on the basis of money. That's healthy. It shows character.

I am especially inspired by young couples with children, who seek the least change possible. They turn down hefty salary increases. They have the strength to say "no" and mean it.

While we can applaud such actions, we are still left with the reality of change over which we have no control. Can you and I stop the clock from ticking? We know the answer.

The truth of the matter is many of us need the stimulus of change. A new job, a new home, a new car, a new dress, or a new fishing pole are exciting. They can motivate.

Some of us change churches and communities fairly often. We can move every three to five years and benefit from it. There are always good people who will love and appreciate us.

One's roots are very important, and I have always been grateful for mine. At the same time, stagnation from sitting too long in the same place is tragic. Change tends to make us grow.

We used to joke about teachers in the same school system over a long period of time. Did she or he teach twenty-four years or one year twenty-four times? You see, there really is a big—very big—difference.

Of course, what troubles some of us who have lived more than a few years is a particular kind of change. It's as though one is unable to become a person of substance. It is a problem.

I have known many persons—and so have you—that seem like leaves caught in a wind. They never land any place for very long. Even when they do land, not much productive happens.

So, how about you and me? Do we have the moral and spiritual sensitivity to have wisdom about change? We must be willing to take it or leave it, depending upon that inner wise man or woman.

11   Examining the Status of Celebrities

"I got to meet the president," he related with pride and a superior smile. It was as though no one else had met him. Get the picture?

Before we cast stones, let's be reminded of our own human tendency to brag. This is especially when we meet someone really important. How many such people have you met?

In retrospect, were they really all that important? Perhaps those who set records have now had their records broken. For a brief moment, they seemed like gods.

Sometimes we get our gods and God confused. We can even discover our lives dependent upon their ongoing greatness. Movie and sports stars fall into this category.

This sort of thing can blind us to their humanity and mortality. We deal solely in images. We keep propping up these images in hopes they will not die.

I suspect for some this seems like a minor problem and possibly not a problem at all. Favorite celebrities help us to cope with life. We need them—or do we?

Some years ago I was invited to St. James Cathedral in South Bend. The archbishop of Canterbury would be there. It was a grand opportunity for someone very interested in Christian unity.

So, I met this spiritual celebrity and visited briefly with him. He was approachable in a kind and warm way. He had the grace of a monarch and the look of a country priest.

He said the biggest mistake the Church of England made was to let those Methodists get away. That chasm happened more than two hundred years ago. That was a fascinating statement to me.

This celebrity had said something of significance in relationship to Christian unity. His historical and theological insight at first was humorous. Then it began to sink in.

Since the earliest of times in the history of Christianity, it seems people have turned away. There have been more splinters than we like to admit. There is sadness in this.

Probably every denomination on the face of this earth came about because of needing to break away. So often mini-celebrities have been responsible. What do you think?

No religious celebrity deserves the place of Jesus the Christ. Stay with the source of your faith. Their names are not John Wesley, Martin Luther, John Calvin, or Pope John Paul II.

12   "Remember When" Is an Important Part of Life

"I remember when" is a common expression for those beyond about fifty years of age. It becomes very important to recall certain people, places, and things. It becomes a habit.

As a boy, I used to spend many Sunday afternoons listening to older adults talk about "remember when." It was boring. Yet, today, I remember it as a fascinating experience.

To a lad in the Blountsville school, it seemed to be a waste of time. What good was accomplished and who cared? Well, obviously for them it fulfilled a need.

In retrospect, it was a way to deal with one's family tree. It was also a way to relate to the past so that connecting links matched up. Friends and neighbors mattered.

Prejudices and false assumptions, of course, are nothing new. While we are generally better educated today, not that much has changed. We have a need to remember when.

There is a certain healing and reconciliation in all of this. The mere verbalizing of someone in relationship to someone else may be a form of therapy. Pity someone over fifty who doesn't do this.

National and world events are not that different. Where were you on December 7, 1941, at the time of the attack on Pearl Harbor? What relative died as a result of this initial bombing?

Where were you the day John F. Kennedy was assassinated in November of 1963? Where were you the day Hank Aaron broke the Babe's record? Examples are almost infinite.

Something deep inside of us requires we piece together certain lives and events. Not everything is to our liking but that doesn't matter. In fact, some things are distasteful.

We human beings do not come and go in a vacuum. We are surrounded by people and things. Even hermits in remote places have or have had fathers and mothers.

Piecing one's life together is not always easy. In prim and proper families, there is invariably the black sheep. But everyone has to have a place of some kind.

I suspect at this very moment there are those putting together data that enables them to understand themselves more fully. I guess that's what it is all about. Yes, I believe so.

The next time you are remembering when, give thanks to God. He did not create you to be a lonely, solitary figure. Others, living and dead, are part of your being. So enjoy them.

13 You're a Minister? I'll Buy Your Coffee Anyway

"**B**oy, is that a good place to eat," the truck driver exclaimed. On most trips, he managed to stop there and fill up a big tummy. He looked forward to it and loved to see it on the horizon.

My experience is that truck drivers always know the best places to eat. It may be fast food or an expensive diner. Nevertheless, they always know where to go.

It seems to be a built-in piece of information that is infallible. Trust them and they will not fail you. When in doubt in a strange area, just ask a truck driver where to get a good meal.

By the way, have you ever noticed how intelligent they are? My education has been enhanced immensely by some of them. They are not merely doers; they are also thinkers.

Some of my most enlightening conversations have been with truck drivers. I have learned not to let them know I am a preacher at first. That has to come later, much later.

I recall this fellow a few weeks ago who expounded on theology. He had insights galore and I listened intently. He really said some powerful things.

Once again this illustrated for me that God is every place. Some of our best preachers are never ordained. In fact, they seldom go to any church. Dirt and grime, some profanity, and wild T-shirts are only the trimmings. What counts is something else. These guys really do some heavy thinking.

Of course, some are openly religious and have lighted crosses on their cabs. That's a breath of fresh air at night on lonely interstates. It's like a beacon.

Perhaps my favorite visit was with a fellow who was cynical of churches and preachers. He told me they were all a bunch of hypocrites. I just listened.

Then he told me he bet I was some sort of a good counselor, and he appreciated my listening to him. Then he swore, burped loudly, and prepared to leave.

He said, "I want to buy your coffee, sir." I said that was a great idea. So he reached for another dollar before paying. Then, he said, "You ain't a preacher are you?"

I pleaded guilty and tried to smile. He said that he just knew it some place along the line. Then, he smiled and said, "I am going to buy your coffee anyway."

14   Exaggerate If You Must, But Know It

"Oh, stop exaggerating," his future wife told him. She wasn't kidding because, after all, she was going to marry this guy. How much exaggeration would there be in the future?

Suppose her husband told her his teaching contract was thirty thousand dollars. The real figure was five thousand dollars less. This meant trouble for making up a budget that worked.

She loved this hunk of a man but all of this exaggerating just had to go. She couldn't very well live her life by having to reestimate everything he said. Surely there was a cure.

Well, the wedding took place and, of course, he tried to impress her family by saying he was on the verge of finishing his master's degree. The truth: he hadn't even started on it. Will this marriage make it?

They are still married and she has made adjustments here and there to account for his problem. Love can cover an awful lot of difficulty. Hopefully, she will still be adjusting years from now.

In all honesty, I don't think we should be all that hard on this fellow. How about you and me? Is there one among us who doesn't inflate something once in awhile?

You have heard the expression "If the shoe fits, wear it." Confidentially, I know some pastors who say they preach to large numbers of people. Just how large is large?

I can remember as a young, ambitious pastor saying I preached to nearly 200. Usually, I was about 10 percent over the actual figure. Would you believe 179 was the hard cold total?

Some years ago I had a wonderful layman who counted our attendances at special summer services on Lake Tippecanoe. He had a unique way of counting. For example: 211 people, 18 ducks, and 4 dogs. Then, he would smile sheepishly and indicate attendance was 233. That sounded about right to me. So, it became a little private joke we loved to talk about.

Now, before you begin to feel smug, try to count the times you practiced the not-so-subtle art of exaggeration. Be honest, now. It happened just the other day, didn't it?

On a more serious side, it is important to know when we inflate something. Otherwise, our self-deception can eventually destroy us. Exaggerate, if you must, but know it.

A preacher was so proud of himself after preaching one Sunday, he confidently asked his wife how many great preachers there were in the world. She dryly said, "One less than you think."

Emotion Boiled Over

The old deacon shouted, "I just want to tell him to go to hell!" He was red in the face and you could tell he was in earnest. He was really having trouble controlling himself.

His wife was in another room but heard the emotional outburst. In fact, she wondered if the neighbors had heard it. They had been married a long time and she was surprised.

After a time, she went to see what was going on with her husband. He was known as a stellar member of his church and highly respected. This was out of character.

He hadn't cooled off much, but she began to inquire anyway. Just who was it that he wanted to go to that awful place? Who deserved fire and brimstone?

It took some doing but he finally opened up. He told her that he was talking about their pastor. The reverend had made a terrible decision and everyone was going to suffer.

His wife gasped and in her finest tones told him he should never say that about his pastor. After all, he had baptized, married, and buried some of the family. She had never seen him that way.

This didn't help much and he emphasized he still wanted to tell their pastor to go to hell. Of course, he had begun to feel guilty by now. He wished he hadn't gotten so riled up.

Well, by now do you feel compassion or disgust? Frankly, I feel compassion because as the saying goes, "feelings are facts." He was a genuinely good man who cared about people.

The truth of the matter is that sometimes, hopefully not very often, a parishioner needs to confront the pastor. If there is both honesty and maturity, it can be helpful. Fear need not get in the way.

Granted, the old deacon might be near the edge. Nevertheless, he needed to get something off his chest. Hopefully, his pastor will listen and grow from the experience.

Let's face it. We have all been very upset towards someone and then felt we should not feel that way. This is especially true in the life of the churches and as we relate to pastors.

The dozens of truly genuine pastors I have known over the years will react positively to such emotion. They may be hurt and seriously wonder why some guy wants them to burn. But, just maybe, they should feel that way occasionally.

Let me offer a suggestion or two. If you want to rant and rave at your pastor, pray on your knees first. Then, you will be prepared for whatever needs to be said.

16   Faith Helps Bind Relationships

She sobbed, "I am sorry, so very sorry." It was a moment out of a soap opera, except more powerful. The young wife and mother was trying to come to terms with a serious mistake.

Only her husband was present and he listened intently and with much disbelief. He was a quiet and hard-working man, who loved her. The man would listen for a long time to his distraught wife. He would say only one word in the entire encounter and that would come at the end. He was a patient man.

Her story was bluntly honest and it caused her enormous pain. Yet, it needed to be told in order for her to go on living. The pressure of her indiscretions had to be answered.

She began by saying she had always wanted a better station in society than her husband gave her. She respected his work ethic and considerate attitude. But that wasn't enough—her husband's love and that of their two delightful little boys wasn't enough. She craved a man of power and prestige. She had from her first years in college.

She did many things right, including caring for him and their family. But there was this niche that had never been filled. She seemed helpless and yet driven.

Then, of course, the right man came along. He wasn't at all like her husband. His looks, his ways, and his manners swept her off her feet in a way that surprised even her.

Soon she began a double life that no one suspected. Certainly her husband had no inkling. Her neighbors and friends saw the family as close-knit, generally happy.

It was just one of those things she kept saying to herself. It would pass quickly and no one would know. But it didn't, and she began to sense she was at the edge of a cliff.

Her husband had to know in order for her to have any semblance of peace of mind. She didn't want to hurt him or their prized sons. Nevertheless, the time had come and she rose to the occasion.

She kept unraveling her story in a flood of tears and grimaces. Her husband's total silence was somewhat disquieting. Finally, her story in all its sordidness was finished.

Through swollen eyes she looked penitently at her husband and asked if the marriage could continue in faithfulness. He smiled. Then, he looked into her eyes and said, "Yes."

17   When Is Church Over?

"When is church over?" a little fellow dressed in his best suit asked his dad. It seemed he couldn't remember when it was time to leave. What signal did the pastor give?

His father explained that when the benediction was given, it was over. Then, he added that was the closing prayer. People bowed their heads and were thankful for the time together.

I guess we have all heard those jokes about long-winded preachers and ongoing testimonies. Well, sometimes it is difficult to tell when church is over. It can be tricky.

As a little boy in the old Blountsville Christian Church, I used to wonder when church was over. Those wooden pews seemed to fight with me. Eventually it was time to go.

Mind you, I knew early on that church was a good thing to do. But when would it be over? The word "benediction" had just entered my vocabulary and had not settled in.

After several months, I did learn some signposts. For example, if we had singing, testifying, praying, and preaching, I thought we were getting close. Oh yes, and the offering.

But my real indicators were found in a couple of men. They were there every Sunday. They also let people know they loved the church and came to do certain things.

One of them was Danny Metsker. Church was never over until Danny shouted at least once. Boy, could he send you right out of your seat at the least expected moment.

19

No benediction was going to carry any weight whatsoever until he shouted. I really kinda' enjoyed the drama. That was especially true when one of the prim and proper ladies shrieked.

I once heard Danny explain why he shouted. He said before he was saved he went around cussin' all the time. After he was saved, he started shouting and stopped cussin'.

Some years later, I discovered that was a really good trade-off. Moving the same energy from bad to good is what helps all of us. Danny's burr haircut remains fixed in my memory.

The other fellow who gave me a clue when church was over was Mr. Conwell. He always said the same thing. Invariably, it was, "The Lord is my Shepherd, I shall not want."

Church wasn't over until Mr. Conwell had said his words. Yes, and church wasn't over until Danny had shouted. So, who needs benedictions when you have fellows like that?

18   A Look Back . . .
Memories of the Great Ones

"**S**he was a queen," the elderly man said as he looked upon his mother's face in death. He remembered many good things about her. Yet, for some reason, he forgot to tell her while she was living.

Really, he was a dutiful and grateful son. He just hadn't recognized and thanked her enough. She was unquestionably a queen in his eyes and the eyes of some others as well.

Have you ever had similar feelings? Well, I have and sometimes it makes me feel sad. More could have been said and more thoughtful recognition given.

I especially remember grandmother Grace Gibson Walradth, who rests triumphantly in the Mooreland Cemetery. Her parents named her well. She was both graceful and gracious.

That lady was a real prize. She is the only woman I have ever known who could do hard farm work gracefully. This was true whether she milked cows or fried chicken.

It seemed to me she more or less glided through her work. Only after she was gone did I learn her secret. She didn't really know she was a queen, but others did.

She had two daughters and three sons. She cared for them with class. Her oldest grandson marveled at her with little appreciation at the time. What a lady.

It was not the work she did that impressed nearly as much as her style. That lady could be gracious around farm animals and piles of you know what. My friends, try doing that.

She had a nobility that no one could confer upon her. God gave her that special gift of being "grace" in ways I still get emotional about. She has been at rest more than thirty years.

So, do you know someone with so much rustic royalty? Better tell her today that she is a queen. There are women struggling in the contemporary world in their private and professional lives.

But I'll bet under today's circumstances there is a queen in your life somewhere. Look around and look carefully. Is she graceful and gracious in trying circumstances?

Ah yes, they are among us, aren't they? Their finesse carries the day and those about them are nurtured. Why wait to pass along the accolades?

Well, Grandmother Grace, that's it for now. Enjoy your queenship. I can think of only one other woman who ranks ahead of you and that's our Lord's mother, Mary.

19

Multi-Faceted Friendships

"**H**e is one person I will never forget," he said emphatically and with a certain finality. I guess we have all had those experiences. Such a person just keeps visiting our hearts and minds.

The imprint is made for whatever reasons. There is no shaking the impact the person has on our lives. The person may be good, bad, or otherwise in our sight, but that doesn't matter.

During my first year of teaching school in Redkey, I knew such a man. He and his father ran a restaurant. It became internationally known. Reservations were two years in advance.

Of course, I am thinking of Shambargers and John in particular. Those were the days before the restaurant was written about in the *Wall Street Journal*. Those were very good days.

While providing our meals, John would tell fascinating stories. His father would look on admiringly. So would Franklin D. Roosevelt, whose picture was featured.

I believe John could do anything. He could have been a chef in the Waldorf-Astoria in New York City. That was common knowledge. The position had been offered. But he would rather make his own salad dressings, wait tables, and do his night club acts for friends. He would rather work in a restaurant in serious need of repair. Yes, that was John.

His personality was, to say the least, charismatic. Sometimes he seemed to have the mystical ways of a Buddhist priest and at other times the meekness of Jesus. Yes, and he could stare like Jack Benny.

One can't help but wonder what he could have been in the world's eyes. I don't think that was ever on his agenda. I suspected he rated teaching his Sunday school class in Redkey over working in New York.

To know John was something like the blind man touching an elephant in different places. About the time you thought you knew him, you didn't. There was always more to know.

What set him apart was there were so many different sides to him. He was part shaman, part comedian, and part teacher. In a way, he was the Robin Williams of Redkey.

Isn't it wonderful that God allows us to know such people as we travel this life? John radiated goodness. He seemed to do so in different languages and even religions.

Most of us are not nearly that multi-faceted and we can usually count our talents on one hand. Give thanks for the John Shambargers. Give thanks for your special place. It is yours.

20

Perception of Greatness

"Who was the greatest person in the twentieth century?" he seriously inquired. Everyone in the room began to respond. Each had his or her point of view and gave it.

It is an intriguing inquiry and at the same time tells a lot about the person giving an answer. Does the greatness mean influence? Does it mean goodness?

I am sure you have picked one or more. You have probably seen some of the lists. If you made a careful choice, you likely drew up certain specifications.

Some look at it in political terms, coming up with people like Franklin D. Roosevelt, Dwight D. Eisenhower, and Sir Winston Churchill. The list can get much longer.

Some look at it in social terms, coming up with people like Mahatma Mohandas Gandhi and Martin Luther King. Quickly you can add names. You might even know the person.

Some look at it in religious terms, coming up with people like Mother Teresa, Billy Graham, and Pope John Paul II. This list can really get long. Who is your choice?

It would take books to look into our subject with competence. Many have already made their choices. Regardless of the answers, the process helps us to put our values in focus.

Some, who are sports enthusiasts, might even choose Babe Ruth, Michael Jordan, or Dan Marino. Maybe Kent Benson or Steve Alford. Some might like Larry Bird, Magic Johnson, or Oscar Robertson.

You begin to see how hard it is to decide on two or three persons. It simply depends on how you approach it. Note that our own values invariably come to the surface.

My strong universal religious inclinations tell me the answer is Pope John Paul II. My understanding of history tells me his name is Sir Winston Churchill. Both are mountains of strength.

John Paul II—in a sense—was beyond Roman Catholicism and was a pope for many with and without labels. Everyone could learn from him. He really belonged to all of us.

Sir Winston Churchill's persistence and fortitude gave the world hope, as no one else during the most hellish moments of World War II. His oratory was a divine work of art. His stubbornness was superhuman.

Can these beacons aid and assist—even inspire—us in the twenty-first century? I believe so. In the case of the pope and Churchill, they model values that are always necessary for mankind.

"**A**ll he ever wanted to do was throw his weight around," the man said. For those listening, the message was quite clear. Here was a man who valued power and influence over others.

We have all seen them. It seems they are usually ambitious men, but sometimes we perceive women the same way. It is a fact of life and adjustment is often necessary.

From a different viewpoint, have you known those who could throw their weight around but who didn't? In fact, they were even expected to do so. Yet, for some reason, they didn't?

I remember a man very well who fit into the category. Not only did he have power and influence, he was handsome. Had he spoken, others would virtually have gotten on their knees.

This fellow was a member of my parish some years ago in Seymour. He came to worship often with his wife and family. You couldn't miss him; his demeanor was that of a statesman.

He was the former governor of the state of Indiana, Edgar D. Whitcomb. He was "class" in the traditional sense. He looked like a governor, senator, or even a president.

Not once in the nearly five years I was in that pastorate did I ever see him throw his weight around. In a way, he even seemed to work at not doing it. I really appreciated him.

Well, how about you and me in our little worlds of power and influence? Is it important we show others we can put people in their places? Let's be honest, dear friends.

A tyrant or overly dominant person can be any place, even at the smallest committee meeting. I suppose the reasons are many. Sometimes such a person poisons the entire setting.

Whenever I am tempted to throw my weight around, a few words enter my consciousness. They are crucial. Sometimes they cause my brain to go reeling for a moment.

They come from 1 Corinthians and go like this: "Love is patient and kind; love is not jealous or boastful; it is not arrogant or rude." That's a wake-up call. It is necessary.

I strongly suspect the best way we exercise our power and influence is with those words burnt into our beings. Then, we can do the work of the Master. Then, our weight becomes positive, even therapeutic.

So why don't you and I, regardless of our perceived importance, flee from the temptation of being Mr. Big or Ms. Big? Ben Franklin once said, "Imitate Jesus and Socrates." Splendid advice.

22   Respect Not the Problem

"**H**e was a difficult man, but I loved him," the son said in regard to his father.

Respect was not the problem. A difference in personalities and generations was.

How many people have you known who were difficult but you loved them? Just maybe you and I are among those considered difficult. Hopefully people love us.

My memory takes me back to a man who I thought, when I was a little boy, was a giant. He must have been ten feet tall in those days. He could do anything and everything.

He was my grandfather Glade Walradth. As the oldest grandson, I seemed to rate a special privilege or two. In retrospect, I believe others noticed this long before I did.

When he took me along to the various livestock sale barns in east central Indiana, I thought I was in heaven. When he gave me a fifty cent piece, I knew I was. Goodness, what good times.

As I walked along with him among the farmers and dealers, I could sense a certain aura. Papaw was somebody. Even in silence, they moved so he and I had plenty of room.

As the years passed, I learned he was very successful. He owned hundreds of acres of farmland and was a very skilled businessman. He was a proud man who relished his place.

Well, yes, people said he was a difficult man, but I loved him. Papaw Walradth was a man among men in a day and time of rugged individualism and all that entails.

Sometimes he just simply outfoxed his competitors. He always walked with his head and shoulders thrown back. His kingdom was there to see and that didn't help some people very much.

He was a sports fan par excellence. He had two sons who put little Center High School on the map. I believe he fought as hard as they did at some of those games.

Only recently a man told me that in his high school basketball days, he had helped rough-up one of the Walradth boys. Well, this was about 1940 and things were different. Basketball was war.

It seems the fellow helping with the roughing-up moved quietly away from the incident. Then, at mid-court he turned to look in another direction and was met with a right to the jaw. Grandfather decided to defend his son's honor.

Was he really a difficult man? It's hard to admit, but I guess he must have been. But I loved him and Papaw now resides in the Mooreland Cemetery as competitive as ever.

23   A Mother's Special Love

"Only his mother could find him handsome," the old gentleman laughed. Well, there were people poking fun at the little guy. Define good looks and he didn't seem to have any.

There were those who tried to hold back their snickers. For the most part, everyone—regardless of age—just smiled or frowned quickly and moved on. His playmates were not very kind.

Well, God bless them. As far as I know, mothers have always found their daughters beautiful and sons handsome. Giving birth is special, regardless. I strongly suspect there is nothing quite like it.

But there is a bigger, much bigger, picture and that is to do with all children. As far as I know, none of them ever asked to come into this world. Maybe you know something I don't.

I sometimes get the distinct impression children are to fit into our plans. Do they know when they are unwanted? Sooner or later, I am confident they do.

I remember so well when our first daughter, Anne Marie, was born. I remember even more so my feelings at the time. I had become a father and there she was precious and lovely.

To be honest, I didn't know what to do. Do you pass out cigars and brag beyond believability? Of course, it was a fact she was gorgeous and looked most of all like her father.

In some sort of crazy, even mysterious way, she was really wanted. Seriously, I didn't have the slightest idea what fatherhood meant. But boy, I never felt that way before.

Do you want your children? Oh, some might be better looking than others, but there are no ugly ones. Love them in visible and invisible ways, noting their positive response.

Am I trying to make too big of a case for the love and care of children? After all, we are civilized people and will do what is necessary. But often the facts are not with us.

Why do people get married? In my mind, certainly one of the top reasons is to have children. From the beginning God decreed husband and wife are to have children. I don't recall that being cancelled.

How we treat our children (ours and others') gives a glimpse of the future. So, how does the future look to you? In truth, a whole nation and society in regard to children are struggling to decide.

24   Softly, Tenderly, Jesus is Calling

"I wanna go home," she said in tones at once both longing and tearful. She spent many years away from where she grew up. It was time to make the trip.

Really, that is a wistful yearning in the hearts and minds of countless people. They remember those early years and want to return to them. It is both emotion and geography.

There is a strong sentimental strain in me that wants to go home. Be honest now, there is also in you, isn't there? Life was different then and truly beautiful, nearly perfect.

Sometimes the expression is very eloquently spoken in a play. Mrs. Carrie Watts played by Joanne Rains in *The Trip to Bountiful* is almost breathtaking. She wanted to go home.

Those of you who missed that play in the Guyer Opera House in Lewisville missed a real gem. Those who attended gave thanks to God. What a masterful performance.

It was brilliantly directed by Darrell Hughes and Susie Phillips. It reminded me of the superiority of a great play over that of television mediocrity. Hollywood comes in a distant second.

So, across this country, there are people wanting to go home. The depth of feeling is distinctly human and points to basic, even primal, needs. Yes, I choke with emotion, too.

As you might guess, I wonder about yet another home. It is spiritual and comes from our need to be right with God. I have heard the stories since I was old enough to know anything.

Some of us grew up on songs like "Softly and Tenderly Jesus is Calling." Remember how the refrain goes? "Come home, come home; you who are weary, come home."

Then, we are immersed in a flood of love as it says, "earnestly, tenderly, Jesus is calling. Calling, O sinner, come home." Will L. Thompson wrote that in 1880. Such greatness.

This is perhaps the most moving of all hymns that comes from revivalist days that are so much a part of fundamental Protestant heritage. This is especially true of east central Indiana. Praise God.

So, to go home has a lot to do with calling it quits here and now. It means going to our real home, near to the heart of God. Our real home is with Him.

Conversion is many different things for many different people. Yet, they all—sooner or later—seem to meet at one point. Each of us desperately needs to come to God, our real home.

25 Life is Just Too Precious to be Lost

"Daddy, I am lost," the little fellow cried out. His daddy was just far enough away that he couldn't be seen. The sun had begun to go down and the sky was darkening.

He was only four and this was his first experience at being lost. It was frightening and brought feelings indeed terrifying. His daddy was nowhere to be found and that was awful.

Of course, everything soon was all right. His father walked a few feet towards his son and picked him up. Tears were dried and a broken world was whole again.

Well, by now you have probably seen yourself. At all ages in our lives we get lost. Someone, we hope and pray, will find us, bringing us back to safety.

I like to think the lost are always found. Reality tells me that is not always the case. Furthermore, I am reminded we are instruments in finding the lost.

Jesus continually relates to God as His Father. It is a father-son relationship. Yes, by now, we have all seen ourselves in our weakness and belligerency.

At various stages and points in our lives, we are lost and desperately want to be found by the Father. Who are prodigal sons and daughters? Frankly, all of us.

Sometimes in our greatest successes we find we are lost. We reach out and do not discover the Father's hand. Instead, we find our other hand, hoping that is enough.

Self-congratulation and human adulation deepen our lostness. Emptiness is eventually the result. The truth of the matter is we are desperately lost.

I am not against success, as long as one's hand is firmly in the hand of the Father. Life is too precious to be lost. We are intended to be found . . . permanently.

Have we grown too self-confident and cynical to admit being lost? Deep-down we want to be found, don't we? The loss of hope is uniquely painful and destroys us.

Maybe we have been dealt a terrible blow in our lives and—in effect—disown God. No heavenly Father would allow such bad things to happen. What does all of that prove?

I cannot really speak for you. I do know that nothing can separate us from the Father's love found in Jesus Christ. Cling to Father's hand until his Son meets you face to face.

26   Just Going to Church Doesn't Cut It

"Oh, he never goes to church," she said in disdain. Maybe she felt she was being righteously indignant. Anyway, those about her knew her agenda and ways of evaluating others.

For her it was necessary to go to church in order to be a good person. My guess is she has more than a few who applaud her stand. Sunday school and/or worship are necessary.

I felt a lot like that until near the time I had finished four beautiful years of pastoring at Hagerstown. With some hesitancy, I had to rethink the whole matter. One man caused it.

He was a church member who came once during 208 Sundays, and that was for a funeral. But his demeanor of generosity and kindness was inspiring. He was editor of the local newspaper.

The man's name was Eddie O'Neel and he was a man of great wisdom. Can you be a spiritual director and not go to church? Well, that sounds a bit contradictory.

I was a budding journalist of sorts in those days. He always seemed to have time to listen to my struggles toward maturity. Sometimes we visited early in the morning and sometimes late at night.

He was always at least one step ahead of me. The truth is that on some occasions, it was more like five or six. Yes, I spent a great deal more time in his office than he did in church.

He kinda bubbled over with wit and wisdom. He always encouraged me. I never recalled a single negative word said against anyone, churchgoers or non-churchgoers.

What he gave to the community, except for his weekly newspaper, was really intangibles. He bent over backwards to assist and help people. Behind the scenes he gave himself unselfishly.

I suspect he would have published his newspaper and done his good deeds with no pay whatsoever. Probably only his lovely wife kept him from doing just that. He was something.

You may be asking what kind of a person can be a model for others and not go to church? That is a very good question. Frankly, I don't have an answer for that one.

All I know is that little fellow with the big smile was someone I never forgot. Maybe there is an unselfish and generous attitude apart from going to church. Yes, I feel the cold stares.

But think about it. Think about the good people—men in particular—you have known who seldom or never went to church. Maybe all of this says more about the churches than it does about them.

"It's a throw away," the fellow said at the supermarket. That was his job. He was to go through the store daily and determine what was to be thrown out.

Sometimes it was in the fruit section. Other times it was in the vegetable section. Then, there were other areas that he scanned to see what was disposable.

After a time he became known as the "throw-away man." When you saw him, you knew something was about to be tossed. He was a familiar figure around the store.

He didn't mind it for awhile, but then it dawned on him how people would remember him. It was important how people remembered him. How about you?

Be honest now, it is important for each and every one of us. The fellow mentioned left the store and found another job that paid less money. He was thinking about his grandchildren.

For some years, I have urged people to write their autobiographies in their later years. Really, about the best way to remember is to read what they say about themselves. That's true.

My advice—if you are beyond sixty—is not to put it off. If you need some help in sentence construction, that's available.

You know, we have that right (and duty) to write down who and what we are. Others may disagree, especially if we grossly exaggerate. Even that does not mean we should stop.

How do you want to be known by your grandchildren, great-grandchildren, etc.? Tell them your story because they will want to know. This is neither vanity nor egotism.

I don't want to be known as a "throw-away man." Do you? Give some serious thought to all of this. You may even decide to change jobs and get another.

Some intelligent people have said to me over the years that no one will care once they have been gone awhile. Not so. There is a built-in yearning to know about ancestors.

I'll bet there are thousands of personal stories waiting to be told out there. Fess up now, you haven't done it yet, have you? Today is the best time to begin.

How long is an autobiography? The answer: just as long as you want it to be. Don't leave us impoverished because you didn't take the time to do what you knew you should.

28   Leaning on the Everlasting Arms

"Leaning on the everlasting arms," the dear lady sang over and over. Then she would emphasize she was "safe and secure from all alarms." Oh, she loved that song.

Every place she went she couldn't help singing it. It didn't matter the time of the day or the place she found herself. It meant so much to her.

One day a fellow, who considered himself quite a theologian, began to laugh at her. He proceeded to point out the words really meant nothing. He scolded her.

Furthermore, this self-proclaimed expert on the Christian faith indicated she spoke of something totally irrelevant. Everlasting arms? Safe and secure?

It sounded very much like the faith she knew and expressed didn't have any credibility. Of course, he told her why. Then, he made a big mistake.

She assured him Jesus was her Savior and Lord. He began to ridicule this as too simplistic and devoid of substance. His studies seemed to find no one that personal.

In tears, she began to point out how she lived her life day after day. His response was one of nonchalance. I guess—in his opinion— if you didn't have the right words, the kingdom was closed.

Then, she mustered the courage to ask him how he lived his life. He gave quite a long and complicated answer that was filled with big words. He thought he was brilliant.

She asked the same question again with great sincerity. He came back with another barrage of words and quoted many sources. Surely there was some way for her to be enlightened.

By this time the dear lady put her head down and told him that he was truly a smart man. Then, she added, "I still don't know how you live your life." Emotional explosion.

He raised his voice and in no uncertain terms told her he just couldn't communicate with her. They had nothing else to talk about. He felt sad she couldn't move up to his level.

There was silence and more silence. He looked at her with pity and felt the poor soul was just sincerely wrong. There was too much she didn't understand.

Finally, she knelt down and prayed that her dear Savior and Lord would enter his life. He laughed. I guess there was an awful lot this bright fellow didn't understand.

29   The World Could Use More True Heroines

"**S**he doesn't have an enemy in the world," her grandson marveled. He kept going over in his mind (and heart) her countless good deeds. It was like a beautiful parade.

She just didn't have any enemies. It wasn't that she was high-profile and received applause often. It was more like someone being a servant in all circumstances.

His grandmother wasn't widely know at all. In fact, beyond her circle of friends and family she was barely known. That didn't matter and it didn't phase her.

I suppose it takes a fair bit of gall to say someone has no enemies. It does sound unrealistic and even bordering on dishonesty. Yet, that was the case.

I knew such a woman and her name was Christie McCall Lacy. Yes, you guessed my secret—she was my grandmother. If she had any enemies, I never knew it.

She was the oldest of eleven children. Her son, my father, was the oldest of her eight children. So, she knew what it was to be born into a big family and then to have one.

In all the years I knew her, I never remember any awards, special recognitions, or even major thank-yous. She simply did her work and lived her life. Duty was enough.

One of her secrets was that she never did any posturing. She was the same lady yesterday, today, and tomorrow. My friends, that is a tremendous gift then and now.

Her own needs were so well sacrificed, I am not certain anyone knew for sure what they were. She met the needs of others, especially her family. What a beautiful person.

Her strength and influence were always present. No one had to tell you that grandmother was pleasantly working behind the scenes. She did so not to hinder but to help.

Sometimes I pray to God to send us more women like her. It seems the world would be such a better place in which to live. They are the modest and skilled humanitarians.

If you have never known such a person, you have missed a great deal. They are the stuff out of which life on this planet is lived at the best. She was a heroine.

Is there some way to honor her today? Certainly a posthumous medal would not be to her liking. However, I do believe she would be thrilled simply if we imitated her.

30   Contradictions of Life
Hard to Comprehend

"**I** just don't understand it," she kept repeating. Then she would weep with a heart that was breaking. Her world had fallen apart and there seemed to be no answer.

Her father was such a kind and wonderful man. She had never known him to mistreat her in any way. He was such a pillar of strength for her and others.

Why did he take his own life? Everyone spoke well of him and loved him, she thought. He seemed to have everything to live for and he wasn't old at all, barely fifty.

She prayed intensely and sought God for answers that never came. How could she go on living with such tremendous burden? Peace of mind kept eluding her.

Sometimes she would fall asleep in the early morning hours on a pillow drenched with her tears. Anger and sadness took their turns. Mostly she just didn't understand.

She kept going back over what she knew of his life. There were no answers. Maybe, in time, as she grew older, all would be clear. The passing of years did help some.

Yet, there were days (and nights) the internal storms of not understanding would come. She had been known to shake her fist in the face of God. That didn't help.

Dear friends, maybe you have been there. Maybe even now there are things in your life's experience you are laboring years later to understand. Well, that's most of us, isn't it?

In my more than forty years as a pastor, I believe suicide is probably the most difficult for people to handle. This is especially true if the person is known for his/her goodness.

When truly fine people decide enough is enough of this life, questions emerge for years and years. It is never easy. Hearts break and sometimes continue to break.

The finest man I have ever known took his own life. Oh, there were warning signs and we had begun to wonder. Yet, he was a religious man and very likable.

I never knew him to be mean or wrongly motivated. It always amazed me how he could turn the other cheek. He was a far better man than I am.

Then one sultry August night he ended his life. Now more than thirty years later, I am still not sure that I understand. He was my father, a very good man, the late Charles William Lacy.

31 — Getting People in Touch with God

"**C**hurch was such a bore today," the young fellow bemoaned. *Who wants to read and recite all that stuff*, he thought to himself. *I want to be where the action is.*

Then, he began to plan the worship service himself. *Forget those old hymns that are outdated. Down with sermons that are dull and entirely too long. We ought to sing a lot, pray some, preach a little, and go for pizza. If something isn't entertaining or at least interesting, why mess with it?*

Of course, we need to have Scripture reading. But do we have to have twenty verses when two would be just as good? Yes, and who cares about creeds and those old Psalms?

He had pretty well put the finishing touches to what he considered good worship. Praise songs, lots of informal sharing, spontaneous prayers, and a ten-minute sermon would be just right.

Now, who really wants to argue with this young man? Some of us, even a couple of generations older, have had similar thoughts and feelings. Frustrating, isn't it?

We are living through some years that are seeing worship in various styles. You may disagree, but I am not negative about that. There is a creative spirit at work.

I would be less than honest to say there isn't a problem. In fact, I know churches that have divided over so-called contemporary and traditional worship. I bet you do, too.

Over the years, some of us have really strained and extended ourselves to meet expressed worship needs. No one is ever completely satisfied for very long. We must keep trying.

After all, who said all worship is to happen on Sundays? Aren't there six other days? Yes, and is there any law against providing two or even three different worship services on Sunday morning?

Granted, we will not all be in worship at the same hour. Did the Lord tell us we had to be? Confidentially, my preference is one big worship service for everyone.

Yet to meet human wants and needs, I have bent in different directions. For example, some years ago in Hagerstown, I did a half-hour "golfer's special" at 7:30 A.M.

When in Indianapolis for the first time, I did a "Methodist Mass." Yes, that caused a stir far and wide. But isn't the point that we are trying to get people in touch with God?

32 — Learning to Survive in the World

"**D**on't mess with me," little Joey would say. He was Mr. Tough Guy. In a way, he had reason to be because his father and mother were seldom at home and, in fact, often drunk.

For him, learning to survive in this world meant first of all taking care of himself. He was eight years old. Dad and Mom weren't around much. He had a younger sister to look after.

The streets of the city about the size of New Castle were what he knew best. He mostly slept at home and checked on his sister now and then. He didn't want her hurt.

He had the street smarts of a teenager. Making a buck here and there was so easy, even he was surprised. He knew who he could count on and it wasn't his parents.

Only one other person made a difference in his life. That was his sister, who would soon be six years old. He would protect her at all costs, and he did.

Even at his early age, he knew how vulnerable she was. No one had better lay a hand on her in a disrespectful way. Some neighbors remarked what a great brother she had.

Of course, in life we always get tested, whether eight or eighty. The little fellow with the tough hide and big heart was no exception. He, too, was vulnerable and others knew it.

Hey Joey, how would you like a bike for your very own? These were older fellows who had been known to deliver the goods. He had always wanted one, so opportunity was at hand.

Funny thing, though, there was a catch to the offer. He didn't need to pay even the smallest amount of money. There was one small favor that was asked and it didn't sound right.

He was supposed to enjoy riding around town, while these older fellows "baby sat" with his sister. He was supposed to leave her alone in the house for a couple of hours.

God only knew where mom and dad were. Maybe at work, maybe at the tavern, or who knows. But the bike really was a dandy and it looked like a gift easily gotten.

Strangely, something began to click in his mind and it wasn't at all pretty. There was this word "molesting" he had been hearing about. God, that would be awful for his sister to live through.

Then it dawned on him not only were they messing with him, they were going to do worse things to his sister. No bike is worth that. Sometimes eight-year-old tough guys become men of honor.

"Is that your final answer?" is a popular question across our land today. It conjures up delightful possibilities of winning large sums of money. It has become a humorous tidbit.

I would like to take that in a much different direction. Surely there is some spiritual value in it. Join me for a time to inspect an age-old invitation.

As wayward people move through life, God woos them to come to terms with Him. At every age, He prods with love. It is as though the question continues to be repeated.

Many are not only reluctant to say yes to the Lord, they are in full rebellion against Him. What is their final answer going to be? Will it have anything to do with television?

At sixteen, a young man is invited to come to terms with his Maker. The answer in effect is "not now." So the lad goes his merry way, immersed in life's experiences.

At twenty-five, much the same answer is given. Many years seem to be ahead of him. His health is good and problems are at a minimum level.

At forty, he has taken a few lumps but nothing that seems severe enough to drive him from pride and self-sufficiency. On with the parade. God is too good to let him be lost.

At fifty-five, retirement is on the horizon. He has been blessed over and over again. Yet, God's voice has taken on greater firmness; that "final answer" thing has become irritating.

At seventy, he remembers a painting he once saw with Jesus standing at the door knocking. It upset him because deep down he knew his final answer would have to be given.

I saw a man years ago reject God in his life all the way to the end. I swear it was as though Jesus was sitting on his doorstep weeping. Think about that.

What is our final answer to the greatest of all invitations? Friends, in honesty, we know some day we will be called upon to give it. This is intensely personal and cannot be avoided.

Do you experience this as old-fashioned revivalistic scare tactics? I hope not. From many years of dealing with people in spiritual matters, I find this is the way it is.

Sometimes the final answer has to be given quickly in youthful years. Other times a long life is given for a response. Well, how about you and me? Please don't put off an affirmative answer any longer.

34

**The Art of Being
a Good Waitress**

"**H**ave a nice day," the waitress said with a big smile on her face. I believe she genuinely meant it. At any rate, it really felt good to hear those encouraging words.

Sometimes I think one of the major ministries performed is by waitresses. The opportunities are there. Some, in fact, make use of them and others are blessed.

Some are skilled at human relations and do counseling in subtle ways. It is truly amazing how they can turn a dreary day into a pleasant one. What's your experience?

There are those who are excellent conversationalists. They can talk about several topics in an intelligent fashion. They can be especially alert to current events.

I suppose by now you have gotten the idea that ministry can be practiced most any time and any place. I strongly believe that. Anything else says God is limited.

But back to those dear ladies (yes, and those men who wait tables, too) who do more than serve the food and beverages. Why not make a promise to tell them to have a nice day? Life can be very unfair.

Not too long ago I was enjoying my coffee and dessert with a newspaper in a well-known restaurant. The waitress says, "I have some people I want you to meet." That sounded interesting.

So here comes this young couple with their friend. They wanted to get married but their preacher wasn't available. That didn't sound good, so I just listened for a time.

To make a long story short, after some counseling, I married them in their friend's home. Frankly, it was a beautiful evening and tastefully done. The moment was a treasure.

Then there was this waitress who tried to pour my coffee while weeping. She and her husband had decided to call it quits. I promised to pray for her and did.

Isn't it a nice day when you can have those experiences and many others? My hat goes off to those people, young and old, who put up with some miserable characters.

Whenever you leave your tip, be generous. Yes, and remember to leave a thank you note of some kind. There's a lot of pain in some of their lives and you just might help.

Give thanks for those who seem to go under-appreciated. Next time you go out to eat or maybe just for coffee, smile at your server and remember my advice. It's up to you.

35   Despite Popular Belief, Mom's Not Always Right

"**O**h, get over it," his mother would say time and time again. Sometimes he thought this was her favorite saying. It seemed like she just loved saying it.

Boy, did he get tired of hearing it. He didn't answer back because, after all, that was his mother. No respectful son would be caught disagreeing with her.

Some months and even years began to pass. Every problem situation was met by her advising him to get over it. He was now in his second year at Ball State University.

One day, out of the blue, he began to cry. He tried to control it but to no avail. His dorm room was small and no one was around and that was good.

For several minutes, the tears came. In fact, it had finally become a downpour and his face was red. How on earth does a man explain this behavior?

Then, the respect for his mother took on a new dimension. It had come time for him to admit that saying to get over it wasn't much of an answer to life. Mom wasn't always right.

The spectacle of a young man in charge of his life crying like a little boy for no reason was humbling. He had repressed so much in his life and the tears were an escape hatch.

Remember in the first year or two of college that some of us cried like our hearts were breaking? Especially for a young man, it is painful. Especially when there is no apparent reason.

Many of us have learned that repression of thought and feeling, sooner or later, causes an emotional explosion. Yes, we are all made much like that. Be honest.

To become mature means to sift and sort not just parental ideas but their emotional signals as well. It is right and necessary to respect parents. But there is more to the story.

Yes, mom and dad are not always right. We know that early at one level of our being and yet at another we don't. How about you and me with our development?

A man or woman can be sixty and still dealing with having to get over it because a parent said so. This requires taking a long hard look at oneself. It is necessary.

Maybe right now you need to come to terms with the tapes playing in your head, put there by well-meaning parents. This is crucial to one's growth. Repressed thoughts and feelings can be very detrimental.

36   The Wisdom of Spoken Love Brings Its Own Blessed Reward

"Let me count the ways I love you," the young man said to his sweetheart. Then, in poetic fashion he proceeded to do just that. It was an impressive expression of love.

They would soon be married. They had known one another for five years and had been serious about marriage for the last two. Their wedding was a natural result of their relationship.

After the date had been set, he remembered the numerous times he had expressed his love to her. It seemed that would suffice for a lifetime. Then a wise man took him aside.

This man explained to him you can never tell your wife too often how much you love her. She wants to be assured often and in different ways. The wisdom made its imprint.

So, before and after marriage he kept right on telling her. She looked forward to his loving words and sometimes told him so. Much happiness was an ongoing experience.

Gentlemen, have you learned this necessary fine art? Your wife wants to know that you love her and she wants not only to hear it, but to see it. These are words of wisdom.

I have not kept track of the couples with whom I have worked who have failed in this area, specifically men. In reflection, there have been many. A few loving words could have saved marriages.

Husbands fail their wives by overlooking or even deliberately refusing to meet such needs. So, you told her last Mother's Day how great she was. Shame on you.

Count the ways you love her every day. Don't keep all that good stuff to yourself. Make it a point to tell her at least twice during the day. I'll bet she listens.

Do you think she will be suspicious about what you have been up to? Well, maybe and maybe not. But the truth of the matter is that's probably not important.

If you are reactivating the habit after some weeks, months, or years, it may take some getting used to. She may look at you in amazement or perhaps with some anger.

The point remains the same. To have a happy and long-standing marriage means the husband is expressing his love to his wife frequently. This works and it always has.

Now, fellows, before you congratulate yourself about meeting your wife's needs, think about something else. What is also obvious about all of this? You, of course, are meeting your needs too.

37   A Gentle, Well-Meaning Cynic

"Who said so?" the old cynic snapped. His life had been one of questioning and challenging. He had become widely known for his way of reacting to any and all statements.

It didn't matter what came up. It didn't have to be religion or politics. In fact, his response might even be after a simple truth was announced and explained.

Well, I am inclined to have respect for such people as long as he or she is not playing a game of manipulation. It is important who said so. Who or what is your source of information?

Healthy minds inquire and question. They want to avoid being duped, especially in matters that really count. Just how do you feel about all of this anyway?

It's hoped that, if two entirely different people make a statement that is virtually identical, we will check things out. We live in a world that requires liars to compare their facts. That's not pleasant.

I have tried and tested some people that I would believe about virtually everything. They would never knowingly mislead you. Their integrity is well above some others we know.

The source of our information is truly crucial. To inquire who said so may be our most important response. Pastors, in particular, are called to be very careful.

It is not rude or disrespectful to bring into question what someone has said is the truth. Now, the manner in which you do that may offend. Hurt feelings may not accomplish anything.

I've always admired those who could point the way to look at something or someone in a different way. We can always say that may be so, but let's look at it another way. This is helpful.

Over the years, I have done sermon talk-backs or dialogues after preaching. This gives parishioners a chance to make inquiries. Sometimes I have heard, "Preacher, who said so?"

I believe the gentle and well-meaning cynic is an aid in our preaching and our lives. He or she has a way of keeping us honest. The person may even be God's not-so-secret agent.

When our world seems to become a lot smaller and we move about quickly, someone who is cynical performs a valuable function. Of course, there are limitations. Yet, think of the benefits.

When challenged, can you support your point of view? It is common sense to be able to do so. I believe the irresponsible talker is among the most detrimental people in our society.

38 It's Never Too Late to Start Anew

"**H**e couldn't seem to get on track," his dad and mother both pointed out. Now, in his late fifties, his parents could recite the years of his failures to make something out of his life.

There were lost jobs, divorces, and run-ins too numerous to mention. In the years since he had graduated from high school, it was one thing after another. Some of it was hard to believe.

Reliable information said there were certain patterns to such misfits. Strangely, he seemed to defy all of this. Not only were his parents baffled, so were counselors he had seen.

Did he drink and/or use drugs? Was he a philanderer who refused to be faithful to his wife? Was he lazy, had he refused to follow orders, had he avoided helpful continuing education?

In all cases, the answer was the same and it was negative. However, he was getting close to retirement and didn't have much of anything—monetary or otherwise—to show for it.

One had to feel sorry for his parents because they were people of means and had helped him in different ways. All was to no avail, and you could see their pain. What was to come of him?

After they were gone, would he end up sleeping on the streets because he had lost all of his inheritance? It all appeared to be a bad dream that should never have happened. But it did.

The only characteristic that looked the least bit consistent in his life was his brief attention span. He was quickly bored. He seemed to be made for jumping from one thing to another.

Not much—if anything or anyone—pleased him for any period of time. The record was there to see. He never tired of moving from job to job and wife to wife.

In what was close to a last resort, a family friend was instrumental in getting him a substantial grant to travel, meet people in restaurants, and record his impressions for submission to a publisher. Big-time gamble.

Off he went, like an inquisitive little boy, going here and there. Across the nation he went, never staying anyplace more than a few days. Notes were taken and he was fascinated.

After several months on the road, he returned happy as a lark. No one had ever seen him so satisfied with life.

At the age of sixty, his book of travel experiences was published and became a best seller. In most cases he had only seen his interviewees once. His parents and friends scratched their heads in utter amazement.

"I always admired his hope in the future," a daughter said in reflection. Her father was now living day by day in a nursing home. Essentially, his life had been lived.

It is painful to watch a parent waste away, even with the best of care. Her father had given to her something very precious. From the time she was little, he had instilled hope.

How else could she have become a physician? When things didn't go well in medical school, he would send a note or make a phone call. Sometimes he would even travel several miles to see her.

Occasionally, he would make dinner plans during her busy schedule. She would almost collapse at the table from overwork and tension. Then he would give his gift.

As he talked of the future, he would speak of hope in numerous ways. Funny, he never really used the word. By the time the evening was over, she was rejuvenated.

Dad was her best cheerleader. She was doing quite well in her profession but missed his cheerleading. She had been in school twice as many years as he, but she thought he was smarter.

Are you and I giving the gift of hope to those about us? It takes an infectious attitude that says nothing is impossible with God.

A conjured up optimism cannot help us. In fact, it may cause us a great deal of heartache. There is power in positive thinking, but it must be genuine and of depth.

The Psalmist says, "The Lord is all I have and so in him I put my hope." At our best, you and I are emissaries of hope. We are not created to spend our lives in despair.

I have found hope many places and among many people over the years. Sometimes people I never expected gave the gift to me at just the right time. How about you?

Pastors need to remember laity can give them hope from time to time. Pastoring churches can be just about impossible. Sometimes it seems as if the pastor can't do anything right.

I believe the most caring and compassionate people I have known have been laity. Often I have wondered why I was paid to minister to them. They ministered to me.

One father gave one daughter the gift of hope. It made a big, big difference in her life. Just maybe you and I can do the same thing for those about us.

40   For the Love of "Hap" and Baseball

"Take me out to the ball game," the four-year-old sang at the top of his voice. He was just old enough to begin to appreciate the thrill of baseball. It was great.

For some of us a lot older than this little guy our memories are a joy. In these parts it seems like you either follow the Chicago Cubs or Cincinnati Reds. Oh yes, the White Sox, too.

My earliest recollections come from a man I adored. He was my uncle, Myron Luellen. No one ever called him by Myron; 99 percent of the time he was "Hap."

Hap was a delightful fellow who loved baseball. Back more years than I like to think, he was the trustee of Stoney Creek Township in Henry County. But that wasn't what drew me to him.

He was a terrific baseball fan and put his nephew under his wing. Would you believe he took me to both Wrigley Field and Commiskey Park? Both are fixed in my memory forever.

What great fun we had! This was the late 1940s and the Cubs were doing then about what they have been doing for more than fifty years. Maybe Sammy Sosa or someone can change the trend.

I must admit it helped a little when we went to Chicago to have another uncle there. He was a Methodist pastor. We stayed in this lovely parsonage and planned our baseball outings.

Aren't uncles great? I have had some great ones, but none like Uncle Hap who shared a love for major league baseball. We spent hours and hours together.

We agreed on everything when it came to the national pastime. Well, come to think of it, that is a fib. His real love was the Cincinnati Reds and mine the Chicago Cubs.

We never quarreled about this and for a very good reason. His gentlemanly ways taught me to be tolerant of another's preferences. I learned arguing wasn't all that productive.

Isn't it a wonderful thing to grow older and reflect on the gifts others have given you? Maybe the Cubs and the Reds will never be in a World Series again. So what?

Love baseball and go to the games or watch them on television. But pay close attention to the things that are being taught. Lives can be changed for the good and permanently.

Maybe there is a little guy, a son or nephew, who needs to go see a big league game. Love the game together. Some powerful and wonderful teaching hopefully will occur.

41   A Father's Deep Despair

"I just don't care anymore," the old fellow said. He was past eighty and his health had begun to fail. But something else was what was really bothering him.

His wife and children had disappointed him over and over again. They didn't share most of his ideals for them. Over the years, they always seemed to be on another wavelength.

He had been a religious and moral man all of his life. Some said he was too rigid and unrealistic in the face of human sin. Others said he was a good man but "out of touch."

Tears trickled down his cheeks as he reflected on his son's divorce and his daughter's unending craving for things. What went wrong? Hadn't they been taught?

Even his wife thought him too old-fashioned and obviously a bore. Yes, a lot of years and increasing pain. At last, it looked like his heart would break in a million pieces.

More than anything else what caused his despair was his third child, a daughter now in her fifties. She appeared to be happily married and was a successful school teacher. Then it happened.

A moral lapse occurred and she became a different person. Other men gained entrance into her life. People were left scratching their heads, especially those in her church.

Of course, gossip is cheap but facts are facts. It got so bad that her friends avoided her. They cared for her but were at a loss to know what to do about her demise.

Her old daddy couldn't help it. He cried and then cried some more. There is often something special about a father-daughter relationship and her expected lofty behavior.

Oh yes, she had children and even grandchildren. That didn't change much for him. You see, she was still his little girl and the hope of a lifetime of faithfulness never faded.

Now, his wife, who was almost as old as he was saw things quite differently. "It was 'just the times,'" she said and wondered why all the hurt and concern. He cried some more. Strange thing about some daddies, they just don't seem to grow up. Surely a fellow who had worked hard all of his life could handle such happenings.

What can you and I say to the old fellow who doesn't care anymore? His despair is real and pieces of his heart are all around. Why not tell him he has been right all along and we deeply love his vanishing breed?

42   Faithfulness to the End Brings Abundant Rewards

"He was a remarkable builder," one fellow said to another. They were referring to this man, now deceased, who built homes that impressed everyone. He was known far and wide.

He worked for the same contractor virtually all of his life. He was held in esteem by many. His homes dotted the area; people came from near and far.

Strangely, when he died the home in which he lived was average and maybe even mediocre. People couldn't quite understand this. After all, he had built it.

One day a story was finally told that surprised the whole area. It was not a pleasant one. It gave a different perspective to the man and his work.

It seems as he grew old and gray, there was a bitterness in his heart. Recognition of his skills did not go far enough. Surely his boss could have paid him much more.

At any rate, as the story goes, he received permission to build his last house. Since it was his last one and surely no one would notice, he cut some corners. It was not his best.

After he finished it, his boss gave him the usual accolades. Then the surprise came. He was given the house to live in the rest of his life.

Since he had little money saved, that's the way it would have to be. So, he spent the remainder of his days in an inferior home he had built. He grew more bitter.

As always, the Word of God sheds a special light for us. Hebrews 6:11 says, "Our great desire is that each one of you keep up his eagerness to the end, so that the things you hope for will come true."

Sometimes we are tempted to do less than our best, much less. Something other than bitterness may be eating away at us. What a shame to fail near the end.

The really good people always have further to fall than those who have compromised their lives. Falling off a pedestal can be very noisy. How sad it is.

We are created to live at our best, right up to the moment we meet our dear Lord. Anything less is unacceptable. Deep down we know this.

So, always build whatever you build as perfectly as you can. Then there will be no regrets. People (and your Lord) will say he/she was faithful to the very end.

43   A Name is of Paramount Significance

"**R**emember my name," she insisted. She was in her late twenties and was proud of her name. It gave her an identity. It provided a way of self-understanding.

Naming a son or a daughter has been very important since the dawning of recorded history. Check your Bibles and even more ancient writings. It is of paramount significance.

Church baptismal records carry authority, as they relate to names given people. Some say they even provide legal grounds. So never underestimate the name given to you.

We were not created to live our lives by being called by numbers. There is more to us than so many digits. Who wants to be known that way, even in today's world?

You may say to wait a minute and consider the power of a Social Security listing. Well, of course, but that is to aid us in the way we live. At the deeper levels, it is not to identify us.

I remember so well after each of our four daughters was born, I called them by their full names. First there was Anne Marie, then Donna Jean, then Sharon Elizabeth, and finally Martha Elaine.

I wanted their names to mean something to them all their lives. They would never be "hey you" or "the one who was the shortest." Aren't names so precious?

The next time you are with a friend say his or her name carefully and in full. It will add respect to your friendship. You will both smile and maybe shed a tear.

When we pass into the hereafter and meet our dear Lord, I happen to think He will call us by name. It will not be like a line of newly drafted soldiers. It will be an unforgettable moment.

If we can focus on the uniqueness of another precious human being, we tend to get outside of ourselves. For most of us, that is positive. Say his or her name with affection and due respect.

I sometimes chuckle out loud as I remember the story of my naming. My middle name was a given and it would be Charles. What would my first name be?

Long ago my mother sheepishly told me the story. She said, "Your father and I tossed around some possibilities. None seemed to fit the occasion or needs."

Then, she said, looking off in another direction, "There was this cute little boy in the neighborhood named Donald." Well, that's not a very auspicious beginning. But it is my name.

44   Good Politics in the Small Town of Hagerstown

"Where's the postmaster?" was a common question about two mornings each week. For about forty-five minutes, no one could find him. It remained a mystery for some time.

One day, someone got the bright idea to call his wife. She chuckled and said he was out having devotions with the Methodist pastor. Between the lines the truth leaked out.

The highly respected Paul R. Foulke, in fact, was having a coffee break with his pastor. Well, yes, I was his pastor in Hagerstown at the time. Paul was a dear friend.

Probably no one knew the town better than he did. Sometimes I wondered if it could function at all without him. He was a great and caring pragmatist.

Those meditations—I mean, coffee breaks—were cherished times. As a matter of fact, that's really how I became a master mason. He worked with me until I memorized the ritual.

In one's lifetime a few people teach you so much and are so loyal, smiles of appreciation come years later. I count Paul among them. His gifts were special.

Perhaps the most profound and helpful gift was the notion of "good politics." You see, when dealing with people there are always politics, good and bad. The goal is to have good politics.

There is the Paul R. Foulke Parkway in Hagerstown at the east edge. It is a fitting tribute. It also provides us a reminder of someone who never sought prestige and power. I am not sure there is anyone in all of my forty-plus years in the ministry who had a better handle on the workings of a town. The highly educated and wealthy couldn't learn or buy what he knew.

He was not saintly, but then sometimes I wonder . . . just maybe his holiness was so unique it escaped all of us at the time. As you grow older, you learn saints come in different sizes and shapes.

So, how is it in your life today? If you have never known a fellow like him, you have missed a great common-sense education. Of course, maybe no one is made that way anymore.

There is a special thing about towns. They aren't cities and don't pretend to be. Towns like Hagerstown and others provide so much in real living. I have served churches in cities, including Indianapolis, but I never found a Paul in any of them. Amazing how the glitter and glow of bigness is often socially and politically deficient.

"I'll be there Tuesday," my dear Grandfather Lacy used to say. He was a plastering contractor and was referring to the day he would be at a new job. That seemed reasonable to me.

As a young teenager, I finished my first summer working with him. There was something about this Tuesday business that puzzled me. We didn't always get to a new job on Tuesday.

So, about Thanksgiving I brought up the matter. Guess what his answer was?

Well, he told his grandson with a glint in this eye that he never really said *what* Tuesday. That was revealing.

He had learned long ago that the pressure of the building trade has to be responded to very carefully. You can't always finish plastering a home on Monday evening. There are too many variables.

Yet, the impatience of people required some sort of an answer. His was not a lie and actually not even dishonest. It was a way of saying, "I will do the best I can."

His reputation as a hardworking and competent plasterer was impeccable. More than I realized at first, he was quite a good psychologist and survivor. Flexibility was an imperative.

Come to think of it, I am not sure how far I could go with such an approach. If a certain homebound lady was expecting me on 2:00 P.M. Tuesday, I better know the date.

While that worked for my grandfather, it doesn't do much for me. It is a different day and time. Yet, in a way we are similar because we both highly value our reputations.

Life is never lived in a perfect world. Grandfather used to say, "If I had a million dollars and no poor relation, I would quit the plastering business." Of course, he didn't have either one.

I don't want to return to a time of more than fifty years ago. My guess is that you don't want to do so either. But give thanks for their "know how" and paving the way for you and me.

Well, I must go do something on Tuesday. I don't know what Tuesday it will be, but it will be important. All of life is that way and thanksgiving is in order.

"**I** just love his style," an elderly lady said with obvious admiration. She was speaking of her pastor. His every word and movement were perfection.

In a way, he was like her son whom she had wanted to go into the ordained ministry. Her son never fulfilled her wishes; he died tragically at an early age.

Her pastor was really something, especially in the pulpit. He knew how to hold the Bible and could read it like an angel. Sunday morning was the high point of her week.

There were those in the congregation who occasionally asked her what he said. This seemed so unimportant to her. She was inspired and thought everyone else should be as well.

Then, it occurred to her to jot down notes on a Sunday or two. She did, and it was painfully revealing. The way he did things was very impressive but what had he said?

Her notes didn't show much in the way of biblical or theological substance. So, she kept on taking notes and would try to remember his main points. Trouble.

After a few weeks, she looked over her words and discovered Moses was a nice fellow. Paul was a nice fellow. And the nicest fellow of all was Jesus.

Sometimes style and substance don't go together. I believe many parishioners in a hurry on Sunday mornings seldom make the connection. The big-ticket item is style.

It is not so much what he said as how he said it. If his suit coat or gown is wrinkled, that's noticeable. If he is in need of a haircut, that's also a problem.

The great preachers, in my opinion, have always put substance above style. Of course, if you can have both, that's just great.

Some of today's great preachers are entertaining and sometimes they are not. Most always, however, they have something profound to say.

At one time in our nation's history, sermons were printed in local newspapers. Individual copies also circulated in many parishes. There isn't much of that today.

Maybe across this land of ours we should free-up pastors, so they have the time to write them out in full. Then they can be reproduced each week. Well, it's a thought.

47 Lighten Up

"That fellow is a riot," an older lady said as she chuckled. He was her nephew. Yes, he was funny and naturally so, as he moved along in his busy world.

For the most part, others appreciated his sense of humor. It was just plain fun to be around him. About everything had a funny side and he found it.

It is amazing what humor will do, even in the life of the churches. Tense moments in committee meetings can be changed. The solution is well-placed humor.

In another day and time, Will Rogers was a widely known humorist. He also had the skill to convey homespun philosophy that counted. Will was a riot.

I was an associate to a senior pastor in the mid-1960s who was a genius. He always had stories to tell and we looked forward to them. He was special.

His name was Don Barnes. We worked together at College Avenue United Methodist Church in Muncie. He taught me that when church people don't laugh, trouble is on the way.

I marveled at how he related to people in a way that seemed almost like a script. A board member would frown and Don would tell a joke. The board member felt better.

Some parishioner would tell him off and he would thank that person for the compliment. You could only stay angry at him briefly. Then, it was obvious he had won . . . again.

When it came to human relationships, he was the best I have seen. He was a senior pastor of the church for thirteen years. Believe you me, that's a long time for the UMC pastor.

There are times when you and I just get too serious.

Remember, now, confession is good for the soul. If we learn to laugh, there are far fewer brick walls in this world.

By the way, have your heard about the town scoundrel who was praised by his pastor at his funeral? His wife stood up and said, "If he had known all those good things were going to be said, he would have died much sooner."

Yes, and have you heard about the big Texan who helped to get rid of his pastor? He was said to have the "hoof and mouth disease." He wouldn't call and he couldn't preach.

Well, how about you and me lightening up a bit (or a great deal). When you go to your next meeting, church or otherwise, take a good, funny story. I'll bet a dime or two it will work wonders.

48   A Father's Love Has Strong Influence on Daughter

"You are so beautiful," a loving father told his twelve-year-old daughter. She was an attractive young lady to be sure. In her father's eyes, she was much more than that.

She responded in a glowing way. That wasn't just anybody who had said that. Her father had looked directly into her face and said the words as only he could say them.

There's quite an important message in all of this. In a few moments, she heard sincerely and honestly what was needed. That wasn't the same as dad's few words.

Women need to hear early in their lives that their fathers find them beautiful. Of course, this means much more than lovely skin and attractive hair. It means the most important man in her life speaks.

Self-image and self-acceptance of a young woman are strongly influenced by her father. Is she somebody important in his eyes? Deep down there is the cry to hear those words over and over.

Soon boy friends are likely to come and go. Dad stays in her life or, at least, he should. He should be the main man in her life until she marries Mr. Right.

I have never understood how any father could be abusive to his daughter, especially in a sexual sense. Surely, he has no idea of the harm he causes. Does he know God knows?

A twelve-year-old daughter needs the warmth, wisdom, and wit of her father. He may not be the greatest man in the world but that's irrelevant. He especially cares for her.

Will she begin to know and relate to other men in the light of her relationship with her father? The answer is a resounding "yes." He must not fail her by refusing to do what is so necessary.

Perhaps the downside to all of this is that no other man will ever measure up to a really good father. Frankly, I am willing to take that chance, aren't you? Say, "Amen."

I guess, by and large, dads are good fellows who care about those young women in their lives. Some, perhaps many, never get around to being direct and open.

The next time she looks at you (with her costly braces), gently touch her cheek and say, "You are so beautiful." Then do it again. Tomorrow and the next day, do it again.

49   Couldn't It Be a Better Way?

"**I**sn't there a better way?" she painfully inquired of her husband. Their little tightly knit family had been dealt a crushing blow. A teenage son had been in a serious auto accident.

The young fellow seemed to have broken every bone in his body. Surgery after surgery was taking place. Would they even recognize him again after all of this?

Mom, after a time, broke down and wept. When she was awake, she cried, and when she drifted off in sleep, she awakened to a tear-filled pillow. Couldn't it be another way?

Her hopes we so high for her son. He had been bright and was hard working. Yes, even his peers poked fun at him for his style of life that left little room for frivolity.

Would he end up being a mere vegetable? Would she have to watch him, day after day, simply exist? Why so much potential had been destroyed she simply couldn't begin to understand.

Her husband, the lad's father, suffered in a kind of quiet desperation. He wondered, too, about a better way. Sometimes he thought instant death would have been much easier.

Then about the same time, after some weeks, both parents accepted the reality of the situation. A very promising life would sit wasting away in their midst. Apparently this was God's way.

I guess most of us who have lived several years have been there, haven't we? *Please, dear God, surely you can do better than this.* That's not sacrilegious, just human.

For some, it is like being in a tug-of-war with God. We think He should change our plight but He doesn't. Prayers are helpful and God is present, but not much changes.

The lesson that some of us have had to learn is that in all situations, regardless of how devastating, there is opportunity for good. Monumental growth can occur. Yes, it happens.

To try to arrange and rearrange happenings is like trying to paddle a canoe across the Atlantic Ocean. The canoe will be quickly swallowed by a merciless, watery grave.

Stalemates and regret can be a terrible waste of time. God hopes we will learn by what He allows to happen to us. Acceptance of reality shows maturity.

So, today, if you cannot free yourself from a tragic circumstance, ask God to take it and make something beautiful of if. Remember to promise to do your part.

50   Selective Listening Is a By-Product of Rapid Living

"**D**on't tell me that," a young mother said to a neighbor. She was deeply offended by what had been said about her little boy. The exchange of words was not at all pretty.

Of course, there was much more to the heated conversation than mere words. After all, isn't that almost always the case? Our feelings and thoughts come to the surface.

In this particular situation it was a matter of the little fellow stealing from the neighbor's son, who was somewhat younger. What was the truth? Who was willing to listen?

The two families lived close to one another; things were patched up weeks later. They had begun to speak again. Relief of tension was much like a rainbow coming into view.

In retrospect, it became obvious that the mother feeling offended had done selective hearing (listening). Have any of you done that? Well, of course, and so have I.

With the rapidity of today's living, this has become almost a disease. As we hurry, we pick up only bits and pieces of conversation and information. It can be serious business.

Being human, we also hear often only what we want to hear. That was true in the case mentioned. The neighbor only wanted to present information, not start an altercation.

What had been heard was the implication that her son was a thief. This set off a chain reaction, and a healthy discussion became impossible. This has happened to most of us.

Perhaps the most important point is "Are we willing to swallow our pride and allow open, unhurried conversation?" Imagined provocation can cause much hurt. What are the facts?

Pause for a moment and reflect upon some human relations that went awry. Then ask yourself about possible selective hearing. Had you subconsciously heard what you had planned to hear?

Now, don't walk away from the potential healing at hand. Pray to God to give you the patience to "hear the other person out." Try to listen carefully.

To be sure, we do not always have the time to listen to someone at length. If it is a serious enough matter, the needed time must be taken—it must be.

Please practice what is being suggested. I believe a much happier life can come about in many situations. What if our Lord only heard our prayers in bits and pieces?

51   Forgiveness Keeps the World from Becoming a Killing Factory

"Forgive and forget," the pastor emphasized in his sermon. He made the point eloquently and parishioners were listening. What he had to say really made sense and they were appreciative.

We all know people who seem to have forgiven others and at the same time hold grudges. The filing cabinet is ready for opening upon the right occasion. Forgiven, yes, but not forgotten.

Forgiveness is what keeps our world from turning into a killing factory. To maintain even a semblance of order and viable human relations, forgiving is essential. That's the truth.

Nevertheless, I want us to look at the positive side of remembering our sins and those of others. Granted the slate is clean and all is well. Perhaps an illustration helps.

It is said through legendary literature that Peter from time-to-time would hear the cock crowing. It was a reminder of him disowning his Lord. He heard it long after Jesus was gone.

The story goes that every time he became overly confident and would show others how great he was, he soon had a strange look on his face. Others asked him about it. His answer is helpful.

He simply said, "When I become less than my Lord's disciple, I hear the crowing. It happens not once, but twice, and then three agonizing times. I remember, and once again become humble."

Peter's experience may not be yours, but it is often mine. The Spirit of the living God jogs my memory and I must again deal with my sins. I find this helpful and healthy.

I don't feel the need to repent but know I am walking towards a precipice. I have been forgiven but need to be reminded not to do something again. That's my experience.

Proverbs 4:23 tells us, "Be careful how you think; your life is shaped by your thought." Later in verse 27, it is written, "Avoid evil and walk straight ahead. Don't go one step off the right way."

Not totally to forget keeps one from going "one step off the right way." Remorse returns and I discover it is there for a reason. It tells me what I don't want to hear but must.

Granted, some will misuse even forgiveness and make it into a curse. Some will take a sin and nurse it until it becomes a lively demon. The devil must gloat.

So, Paul puts it all in perspective: "Put all things to the test: keep what is good and avoid every kind of evil" (1 Thess. 5:2). Sometimes to remember is the very best thing you can do.

"**M**an overboard!" the sailor shouted at the top of his voice. The lad had fallen into the cold northern Atlantic Ocean. Would he be retrieved before death came?

The "old salts" of the U.S. Navy knew how serious this was. Only a few minutes were available to save him. It was stormy, the waves were high, and visibility was zero.

Before the storm had subsided, three men had fallen into the Atlantic. It was a neighboring ship, so some of us were greatly concerned. We awaited the news.

Some days later, all three were washed up on the eastern coast of the United States. It was a sad day as ships and sailors all around received the news. It was peace time.

Soon thereafter, I became a chaplain's assistant and had moments to reflect on the experience. It was in the mid-1950s, not a time calling for much bravery or heroism.

We don't have to be at war for bad things to happen to priceless human beings. All three men were young and probably had most of their lives ahead of them. People do slip away from us at unexpected times.

Without sounding preachy and overly cautious, I learned in the so-called "best of times" the gospel message must be communicated. When we are healthy and affluent, we can be deaf and blind.

Of course, I am speaking spiritually. One writer said years ago that America can handle hard times, but they can't handle affluence. In a way, that is true. It is easy to lose perspective.

At a deeper level, we can learn much about ourselves. We can spend entirely too much time on economic and material matters. Life becomes little else and we are spiritually impoverished.

Spiritual tragedies happen all around us in times of peace. We can completely miss the significance of them until much later. This is because we think all is well, but it isn't.

There may be no guns booming or submarines lurking but men are falling overboard and drowning or freezing to death. The devil has a brilliant way of rocking us to sleep, thinking all is well.

Followers of Christ are not called to be prophets of doom. After all, it is the Good News we preach. But, let's face it, sometimes we allow our message to be compromised, and that can be tragic.

First Peter 5:8 says, "Be alert, be on watch. Your enemy, the devil, roams around like a roaring lion, looking for someone to devour." Our most dangerous moments may be when all seems to be well.

53 Physical Size Not a Qualification for Character

"Little but mighty," he said of his younger brother. He stretched to about five feet, six inches in length. Soaking wet, he might have weighed all of 130 pounds.

Most of us men think in terms of wanting to be at least six feet tall. Then, 180 pounds is about right. A couple of generations ago that would have pleased most of us.

Of course, we all learn sooner or later that physical size can be very misleading. It is said that John Wesley, the founder of Methodism, was barely over five feet and weighed 135.

James Madison, one of our presidents and founding fathers, was about the same size. As both theologian and politician, he gave much to us, especially in regard to the Constitution.

A lot closer to home, I remember a basketball player years ago. He played for the old Center Spartans (now Wapahani). He was Willie Johnson and could touch the rim above others several inches taller.

In pro basketball, think of Bob Cousy of bygone years and John Stockton currently. Both were physically small men. Their greatness seemed to come from limited stature.

There is wisdom in all of this. For one thing, never underestimate your competitor or adversary. Remember, Joseph Stalin, the communist dictator, stood on a box at parades to appear much taller.

For another thing, remember there are many different ways to measure men and women. A quick assessment of a person can be so inaccurate that it becomes totally laughable.

Lou Boudreau, Hall of Famer at Cooperstown, was observed as a prospect by the Chicago Cubs. The observers said his hands were too small to ever make it in the big leagues, so he went elsewhere.

So, how about you and me? Maybe you are being hemmed in by size, looks, or something else. I would take a careful look at what is holding you back and do a bit of pondering.

Back in 1950, a teacher told those of us graduating from high school that there was no one of college caliber in the class. There were only sixteen of us, but we decided we were not going to hold still for that.

So, two of us set out to get a degree from college and do graduate work beyond that. We were motivated and no one—not even a popular teacher—would limit us, though we may have appeared to have nothing on the ball.

Such an appearance would not defeat us. So we both managed to earn doctorates some years ago. My classmate was the late Dr. Charles O. Jordan who was a prominent superintendent of schools.

54   This Romeo Had a Lot to Learn from "Dumb" Pastor

"**A** ladies' man," she said under her breath. She was referring to a fellow known far and wide. He was attractive to women and he loved the enviable stares that came towards him.

Well, to be honest, he was a handsome fellow and had personality plus. He was still reasonably young and the magnetism had not lessened. Never mind he was in his fourth marriage.

As he was going about his clever ways, a pastor in a small church began to converse with him. Mr. Romeo thought no pastor from a small church knew much. That was a mistake.

Their conversations at first were few and far between. None of them lasted more than five minutes. That's the way things went for a long time. Then, seemingly by coincidence, they spoke at length.

The pastor, who really had neither office nor study, met him for an afternoon coffee break. So, they sat in a truck stop for awhile and then for most of two hours. It was a time of enlightenment.

The fellow managed to communicate his popular and productive ways with women. According to this man, the pastor spent too much time reading the "good book" and needed a more worldly point of view.

For several minutes the reverend just listened, and then he began to feel a sense of anger. After that, pity came. Finally, he silently asked God for the right words to speak.

For someone spiritually sensitive it became evident that Romeo had no respect for women. He thought he was using them. He didn't love or even like them in any serious sense.

They were good for one thing and that was to bolster an ego, devoid of real strength and integrity. Little by little, the "dumb" pastor revealed all of this to him.

It appeared no one had ever disclosed all of that to him before. Could these women be using him? What a dreadful thought this turned out to be, and more (much more).

How could some uneducated preacher in an obscure church say anything important to him? A jolt came when he realized his romantic greatness might not be that at all.

After some sipping of his coffee with his eyes buried in the salt and pepper shakers, he looked up to see a loving and non-judgmental pastor. His face was like that of Jesus without a beard.

So, Mr. Ladies' Man, who had bragged about his conquests, had at last been told the truth. He didn't like it very much and sat in disbelief. The pain was great but the loving power of the living Lord was greater.

55   Reconciliation Brings Peace, Forgiveness, and Joy

"Leave things the way they were," she cried out. Then, there was sobbing that seemed beyond control. She thought sure her heart would break in a million pieces.

Her father had died and then a couple of years later, her mother, also. She loved them and always had. They weren't perfect people, but they were very good to her as far back as she could remember.

Their deaths were hard enough to take, even though both had passed their eightieth birthdays. But this subsided because of the pleasant memories filled with gratitude.

She and her brothers inherited the substantial family farm. In fact, it exceeded three hundred acres of fairly good land. After marriage, her dad and mother never lived any place else.

She loved the place. It was hallowed ground and now she wanted to take her shoes off every time she stopped by. There was so much love for that home and land.

Her brothers were good men and loved their sister. However, they did not see things the way she did. They, too, loved the property but were businessmen and not all that sentimental.

She vehemently disagreed as they moved towards selling it for top dollar. One son had the final say and was honest as the day is long. He felt great sadness.

He tried to tell her the past was the past and their parents had gone permanently from this world. Frankly, this didn't help her much at all. She called him names that she later regretted.

The farm was sold and the division of money was in equal shares. She seriously thought about suing them and then—almost miraculously—decided not to.

In her anguish, she kept wishing things had stayed the way they were. Oh, Dad and Mom were gone but, at least, she would have the farm to imagine them walking about.

After a time, she realized that her lovely home would go to her children and she wasn't certain how they would react at her death. It was sobering. Reality dawned.

She hoped they continued to love her regardless of whether they kept the home or not. Yes, they had to live their lives and the last thing she wanted was to be in their way of happiness.

No more crying and sobbing, except in gratitude. She made peace with her brothers. To her surprise, they shed more tears than she did and the angels sang.

"Won't somebody help me?" a twenty-year-old college student pleaded. She was finishing the second year at the university. It seemed she had lived an entire lifetime in about two years.

Living away from home was frightening at first and then it gave her a sense of accomplishment. She loved her parents and two brothers. Yet, she learned to live apart from them.

Dorm life was sometimes boring and lonely. It was also satisfying in that she had made some new friends. Once in awhile they partied and laughed their heads off.

Professors ran the full gamut. She learned so much from some and so little from others. All in all, her education was coming along. She felt some strides had been made.

But there was this enormous problem that kept getting bigger. Some would call it a crisis of belief. Give it whatever name you like, it had become consuming.

Her upbringing had been in a conservative but not closed environment. Her church had well-defined beliefs but the people were charitable and did not consider themselves the only Christians.

Her plea for help came from the fact she had fallen in love with a Muslim. He prayed five times each day in the traditional Islamic pattern; she admired this.

He was kind to her and there was a high level of respect between the two. But all was not well.

He wanted her to share in his religion and expected her to convert to it, becoming more and more insistent as it became obvious marriage was a real possibility. She stalled for time.

Finally, all she had the strength to do was to plead for help. She had no answers. It was very stress-filled because he was a fine man and loved her, yet he had made it plain he would never become Christian.

I suspect by now many of us would like to say, "Well, I have been there and done that." The truth of the matter is that most of us have not. Can we even begin to help her?

Having spent many years in Christian unity and inter-religious dialogue, I am still not sure what to say. Many of us only had to decide to be Methodist or Baptist, but not her.

I do know a harsh and rigid "no" to his faith is not apt to help. I also know Abraham is a father to Jews, Christians, and Muslims. Almighty God hears the prayers of all three.

57 You Make Me Feel So Good

"**Y**ou make me feel so good," the grandfather told his favorite granddaughter. He was nearing ninety years old and his health had begun to fail. She wouldn't allow him to get down on himself.

Every day that she walked in that nursing home—and that was often—he received a precious tonic. It was as though he became the most important man alive. Oh, how he relished her visits. Always there were the compliments for the past and encouragement for the future. He was a very important person and no one could say it better than she.

As she walked into his room, it was as though the sun had come up. The clouds, especially the dark ones, all drifted away. A taste of heaven here and now was experienced.

His granddaughter was skilled and there were those who insisted she knew how to push all the right buttons. Some even criticized her for being manipulative.

Yes, there were even those who inquired about how much money she would get at his demise. A couple of people in her own family were the most critical. It seemed no one could be that kind for the right reasons.

Of course, they didn't really know the dear lady's heart. She genuinely loved her grandfather. The last thing she wanted to do was be hurtful to him or herself.

She recognized the talk that went on. Her motives were continually questioned, but that didn't prevent her from wanting to make him feel good. She persisted.

Days, weeks, and months passed. The story was the same. He gave God thanks for her, told everyone in the home how great she was, and enjoyed every minute of it.

As is true of all of us—sooner or later—the death angel pays a visit. His health greatly worsened and he no longer knew her every time she visited. She didn't stop coming.

Then, the family was called and they knew Grandfather was about to go the way of all flesh. Most showed up, including the granddaughter. The end came.

As in all such situations, personal items must be accounted for. Usual procedures were followed and his will showed every son and daughter received equal shares.

Some just couldn't believe his favorite granddaughter was not mentioned in the will. But they did find a very old billfold with her name on it. Inside, a note said, "I will see you in heaven," and there was $1.37.

58   Revival Made "Real" by Troubled Times

"There is no religion in that church," Farmer Jones insisted. Even though it was his church, he didn't go very often. It was too cold and people really didn't mention Jesus much.

Actually, it was a mind-set that told the preacher worship was to be over at 11:30 A.M. every Sunday. This was so that everyone could be on his or her way and they could eat on time.

It was 1940, and Franklin D. Roosevelt had been elected for the third time. That didn't set too well with many in Indiana because a native son, Wendell Wilkie, had been defeated. Within months everything seemed to change in America. Pearl Harbor occurred with all of its horror and loss of life. We were in a fight for our lives, and our sons began to go to war.

Soon some of the sons of the church were headed for battle. The Sunday before three of them left, the church with no religion suddenly became alive. The whole mood changed.

For the first time in some people's recollection, they gathered one by one at the altar or communion railing. They were there to bid these young men good-bye. Everyone knew everyone else.

Most were on their knees for the first time in recent memory. No one looked at the clock to see how close it was to 11:30 A.M. The pastor was treated as more than a hireling.

They prayed and they wept. Those farm boys were their flesh and blood. They were not perfect but no one outside of the church walls had better say so . . . not at that moment.

Yes, there was religion in that church on that unforgettable Sunday. The old, the young, and middle-aged were in one accord. There was no time to complain about anything.

It was an event etched in history and most likely made one of the galleries of heaven. Some were stunned and found a permanent piece of themselves. They praised God.

The church was changed during those war years. The three young men fought in the southwest Pacific, Germany, and France. All came home alive but two had been wounded.

They reported upon returning home they were scared to death until they began to remember the Sunday that religion came back into the church. Then, their spirits grew calm and confident.

The church is still open and active. I am told that since that Sunday, now more than sixty years ago, religion is still in the church. Our Blessed Lord says, "I will never leave you nor forsake you."

59 "God Bless America" a Song to Sing Joyfully Every Day

"**G**od bless America," the old fellow named William said with great respect and emphasis. Then he began to sing that greatly moving song. People listened as he sang his heart out.

Well, he wasn't much of a singer. But nobody cared. People smiled and encouraged him. Even if they had not done so, there was a consensus he would sing anyway.

He liked being with his friends there in his favorite greasy spoon. He was so happy, he bought a full round of coffee for everyone. Then they cheered him on some more.

He was one of the very first ones to be drafted for World War II. It seemed like only a couple of years ago he had spent some days and nights in fox holes.

His war experience gave him the great desire to keep on singing that song until he was laid to rest. How he loved the Untied States of America. For sixty years that had not changed.

The truth of the matter is that while he wasn't much of a singer, his friends listened intently. He just kept on singing it and eventually chills were running up and down their backs.

Old crusty Charlie was never known to cry about anything or anyone. But this morning was different. Tears began to slip down his cheeks and onto his bib overalls.

It was like a moment that had dropped out of heaven. No one had really planned it. Yet, they all felt the breeze that made the Stars and Stripes magically beautiful.

By the time old William was getting a bit hoarse, everyone began to look at everyone else. There wasn't a dry eye among the fifteen or so people. There was a radiance in their smiles.

For those moments God had been powerfully among them. God had treated them to a special spiritual experience. No one said much about churches and religion or philosophy.

What they did do was to drink deeply of their heritage as Americans. It was such a precious privilege. Their patriotism glowed on their faces and everyone thanked God.

Sometimes I wonder why we ever complain about anything or anyone. We live in the greatest nation on the face of this earth. We should sing "God Bless America" every day we live.

Show your patriotism. Let yourself go and sing that great song at home, in church, or in your favorite restaurant. Better still, sing a few lines as you get up in the morning and before you go to bed at night.

60   Thanksgiving and Praise First on Humble Hearts

"Turn that thermostat down," a lovely lady sitting in a sanctuary told the usher. It was just too warm in her church. Everything else was fine but it was entirely too uncomfortable.

That usher told another usher and they conferred for a time. One of them, only a few minutes before that, was asked by a parishioner to turn it up. What were they supposed to do?

All across this land of ours I suppose that goes on most Sundays of the summer and winter. Ushers and boards of trustees are the ones who take the flak. Sound familiar?

Occasionally, a pastor is brought into the consultation. If the church is small, he may be brought into it right away. In some situations, he may be both a custodian and usher.

One pastor whose church was averaging two hundred worshippers each Sunday suggested something that wasn't very smart. He moved at the next board meeting to buy two hundred individual thermostats.

Of course, he wasn't really serious and wanted to lift up the humor of everyone trying to get the temperature exactly right. The board members took offense.

One member even shouted out they had a very insensitive pastor who didn't care about them. He was just concerned that the parsonage was perfect for him, his wife, and family.

While I am subject to the hot and cold like every other human being, it seems to me we miss the point. For example, I would have a lengthy prayer of thanksgiving before any complaint.

After all, we are so privileged to be in the churches of our choice. In many cases, they are beautiful and practical buildings. Our dedication has built them.

In short, let's tell God how very grateful we are to have freedom of religion and the opportunity to worship together. So many situations are helped by prayers of thanksgiving.

Of course, if it's so cold icicles are forming in the baptismal bowl, the thermostat should be set up. Likewise, if it is so hot you can bake a cake on the altar table, it should be set down.

Well, folks, I don't know about you, but as for me and my house it's going to take an awful lot for me to complain about the temperature in my church. Surely God is able to see us through.

Maybe one day the Bible schools and seminaries will have a class called 101 in Temperature Setting for Those Who Want to Succeed. In the meantime, carry a prayer of thanksgiving in your pocket.

61   A Person with Joy is Truly Wealthy

"A tender moment," the young bride said. Tears were in her eyes and there was a radiance on her face. If you could bottle and sell all of that joy, you would be wealthy.

The moment was at the end of the wedding ceremony and they were ready to embrace. They paused momentarily and that made the occasion all the more beautiful.

We pastors are so privileged. We get to be closer to them than anyone else, except God. We get to watch the expressions on their faces, especially the bride's.

The thing I have witnessed most often is the joy given birth by hope for the future. Some brides' faces are so expressive. I don't remember seeing any of them frown.

By now I suppose some of you are beginning to ask questions. For example, if there is all of this impressive optimism at the outset, why are there so many divorces?

I always count it a great gift to share in those precious moments. But, like many of you, I can't help making that same inquiry. The reasons are many and complicated.

However, let's never dwell on the failure of marriage but on the promise of happiness built upon real love. We must not sow the seeds of failure as they stand there gazing into one another's eyes.

Staying married today can be really tough. I am not one to make excuses for any marital breakup. Through numerous counseling sessions, planned and unplanned, compassion must be allowed.

Confidentially, every couple that I have ever married who do not make it causes my heart to break. I can still see the joy in the bride's face and the anticipation of many years with her husband.

Temptations come and go. People come and go in their lives. To live near parents and loved ones may not help at all. Living hundreds of miles from family and friends emotionally close to you may seem irrelevant.

But the beginning joy, dear friends, is magnificent to behold. My experience tells me in nearly all cases it is genuine. God is blessing the marriage and seeks to grant fulfillment in it.

Let us continually pray to God in tears that somehow and some way the radiance in brides' faces across our land will no longer fade into cynicism and defeat.

Husbands, when you look into the eyes of your bride, pray that you will always love and cherish her more than any other women. And now we have made some progress.

"**H**e forgot where he came from," he said with a mixture of sadness, anger, and ridicule. It was directed towards a young fellow who left the community and made good.

The man saying the words was loyal to his family and community. The problem was that he had lived in the same place too long and wasn't ready to admit his narrow understanding.

It's a common problem, isn't it? Someone moves away as a young man or woman, and becomes successful in a different environment. It really is an unnecessary situation.

Many of us move away. If you are a United Methodist pastor, you keep on moving and experience several different communities. I have always seen this as a positive experience. Each time you move, new opportunities open and different people influence your life.

Of course, if you are reasonably successful, there are always people who show ill-will. For some who have lived their lives in the same community for many years, anyone who looks bigger than they do is seen as arrogant. That really is a shame. It says a number of things.

In the first place, just maybe we are dealing more with a basic inferiority complex on the part of the accuser. That may have a sting to it, but that is a truth.

In the second place, surely there is room to accommodate all our friends, especially those with whom we have grown up. There is room for everybody, including successes and failures.

In the third place, we may be widely read and spend considerable time on the Internet, but we may not have lived in other communities for any length of time. Living with different people is stretching.

Those who provide stability and talents for one locality over many years are not to be immediately labeled as shallow. Quite the contrary is true. They deserve big "thank-yous."

This all calls us to recognize we need to appreciate one another and not be judgmental. Give thanks for everyone and don't try to stuff someone into a category.

By the way, just changing geographical locations does not guarantee growth and openness. Sometimes people just move their prejudices intact with them.

So, where do you come from? That's not as easy to answer as you might think. It deserves serious thought over a period of time. My guess is that you will be greatly surprised at your answer.

63 Respect is Absolutely Necessary to Complete the Ministry of God's Servants

"**O**h, call the preacher," the elder snapped. *"Surely the man or woman ordained of God could take the time and energy to deal with the matter. After all, the preacher is paid a salary to work for us."*

I wished this wasn't heard and acted out so many times. Of course, the words are sometimes different, but the attitude is the same. The preacher is an employee.

In fact, he is a kind of hireling who knows on which side his bread is buttered. It is never a pleasant state of affairs. It smacks at ways, in my opinion, that are questionably Christian.

The bigger issue is how can the man or woman of God be faithful to the God he or she serves *and* cater to the whims of people? In truth, it is a very difficult matter.

Those of us who minister in the Untied Methodist system are appointed to churches by bishops and district superintendents. Pastors and pastor-parish committees offer their views.

This is quite different from the churches in which I grew up. In them, there was a strong congregationalism. It was possible to be hired and fired in a matter of days. This didn't appeal to me.

There are many variations to the systems mentioned. Certainly, not one of them is perfect and free of human sin. And let's face it, we all like to have our ways.

What has concerned me for many years is the respect absolutely necessary for doing meaningful ministry. The office or position of pastor is very important.

We cannot function as compromised people who succumb to power groups or individuals. The loss of authority and dignity under those conditions provide jokes.

The jokes are usually both in and outside the churches in question. How can hungry and thirsty souls be attracted to those who treat their pastor like a handyman? Ouch.

Granted, some pastors are not as sensitive as they should be to human need. Granted, some are only a little above the level of scoundrel. But let's be more positive.

Christian people are all God's people. Pastors and people are to relate to one another with deep respect. Yes, they are supposed to love one another. That's what the Scriptures say.

Please treat the office of pastor with respect and dignity. He or she is supposed to be your servant under God.

64   Healing Forgiveness Flows From an Open Heart

"They didn't know my daddy's heart," the oldest daughter lamented. He was gone and her mother, brother, and sister were reading through the cards and letters conveying sympathy.

The daughter's expression about her father was provoked by the family's critical attitude towards his life. She had just turned fifty and reflected on his life.

By being the oldest of the children, she had a special relationship with him. Not even his wife, her mother, knew much about their daughter-father conversations.

His family saw him as a man who went to work, spent time fishing, and largely ignored them—except the one daughter. Only she really knew what was inside him.

For example, she remembered how, years ago, he had asked her to take a walk with him. He cried about his son's drinking problem and wondered if God had heard his prayers.

Then, he told her something else no one knew. Every morning he drove to the factory early and sat in his car for several minutes, praying for his wife and family, before he had to go face a strenuous day.

And then he confided in her that he loved all of them so much. It was awfully hard for him to share that. Only with her did he feel comfortable enough to say these things.

Among the other times, she recalled his broken heart when her sister's marriage failed. This time he sobbed and said it must be all his fault. Why didn't he see it coming? He should have done more and hoped God would forgive him. In fact, in her presence he asked for forgiveness, as he chokingly said the words. She held his hand.

On the brighter side, there was the time he missed her sixteenth birthday party. She was devastated, until a few days later he came to her and told her how very proud he was of her.

Alone, he hugged her and reassured her that he loved her even before she was born and had prayed for her future. He had saved some money for her college and told her that it would be hers at the age of eighteen.

His wife never knew any of this because they were not close. She let everyone know there wasn't much to him, except a weekly pay-check that never went far enough. They didn't know her daddy's heart and he was too timid to let it show. I have known many men like this.

Gentlemen, your loved ones need to know your heart. You will be surprised at the healing that can take place.

65 The Amazing, Mystical Knowledge of a Mother

"Mom is making truth again," fourteen-year-old Billy said under his breath. He had seen it before and began to be amazed by its power. It was not obvious to everyone.

As a little boy, he always noticed his mother was right. That was good and the way it should be. He found security in that and slept well most every night.

Then he began to mature into a perceptive person and carefully watched what went on in the family of five. How could his mother always be right? It was fascinating.

Well, mothers do have a way, especially with their children, of making truth. There seems to be a built-in mechanism that sifts and sorts. Before you know it, she is right again.

Billy was sometimes astonished by all of this. After all, she couldn't know everything that was happening in the family. Yet, it certainly looked like she did.

What he had discerned is a special gift of mothers who are close to their children. They have answers no one else has. How they arrive at them is often hazy and even mystical.

Think what enormous power that is. The molding of little minds is part of this fantastic gift. If you want to know what the truth is, go find Mom and talk to her.

I have observed this at work in many families. It is a marvelous work of art and, frankly, she is the only one capable of such a feat. Sometimes men just gaze in surprise.

To be honest, there is also a down side. When anyone can make truth, the door is left open to the blurring of right and wrong. Strangely, wrong might become truth.

Lies and deceits can get in the mixture. Prejudices can be built-in. Old enemies can get what's coming to them. Fathers and husbands out of favor learn the hard way.

It is truly an awesome power that mothers have. The responsibility is also awesome. I mean who would even question her truth? It is a delicate matter and very important.

I like to believe that anything that comes from mom's mouth is the pure and unvarnished truth. I am a traditionalist and a great respecter of moms, even though sometimes disappointed.

Well, Mom, I hope and pray your truth can stand the holy light of the living God. Millions depend on it. We give thanks for your light, but we also pray you will always be totally truthful.

66   A Time of Giving Thanks for the Little Things in Life

"Be grateful for what you have," his daddy told him. It was a pleasant little command that carried a major message. He was sixteen and his daddy was forty-one.

To a teenager, that seemed like some old-fashioned stuff that went out with the first George Bush. He didn't have enough of anything and he would get more and soon.

Settling on a philosophy of life was something that didn't interest him at all. He would live for another sixty or seventy years. There was plenty of time to talk about this.

The world was one big opportunity for those who would not be limited by catch phrases. No one who is sixteen should be limited by anything or anyone. It's all a matter of taking what you want.

Some of us a lot older than this young fellow and some older than his father soberly remember our teenage days. Were we that much different? Well, yes and no.

I don't remember being ungrateful for what I had while growing up in Henry and Delaware Counties. Thanksgiving Day was a favorite of mine. Of course, food had something to do with that.

What I do remember is wanting a lot more than I had. If I could just play basketball like my uncle Bob, what a thrill that would be. Well, I was too skinny and timid.

Those of us who grew up in the 1930s and 1940s didn't want money as much as we wanted to be somebody. Not that money was unimportant, mind you. Yet, that didn't quite get it.

I seriously believe my generation was both grateful for what we had and, at the same time, wanted more. We were ambitious and individualistic. "Just give us a chance," we said.

We were willing to work, so it was an insult for someone to give us money and we not work for it. I guess it was a matter of growing up a certain way—and lots of pride.

Surely we can be grateful at any age for God's blessings. Surely we can rightfully want more, so we can develop and be more productive. The key is spiritual.

Some of the most ambitious people I have ever known were truly good persons. Do you know why? My answer is a simple one and I am convinced a correct one.

Ambition and the Spirit of the living God can be harmonized. We achieve in order to benefit others. God is in control and that makes all the difference in the way we develop.

67 Christian Love is Sometimes Spelled "T-o-l-e-r-a-n-c-e"

"Every time I feel the Spirit," she shouted. It was one of those precious times of much emotion in her church. Worshippers were in the aisles and there was a sense of God's presence.

Hymns were sung with gusto and testimonies were given. Hands and arms were lifted up to the heavens. Tears flowed freely and most everyone said the tears were for joy.

For those who found meaning in such experience, it was the high point of their day. For a time all cares seemed to float away. The supernatural was in control.

There were those in a church down the street who didn't care for any of this. They loved an ordered service with meaningful liturgy. Sometimes people in the two churches debated.

No one ever really got angry, even though in the work-a-day world they were sometimes doing a job side by side. It was a matter of preference and meeting needs.

Really, despite the chasm between the two forms of worship, they were civil to one another. Those who observed this outside the churches thought it quiet amazing.

I wonder about you and me. Have you measured your tolerance level recently? Would such diversity upset us, as we go about our comfortable ways in our churches?

Sometimes it is so amazing what upsets those who claim the name of Christ. It seems a darkened veil comes down. Criticism is full-blown and explosive.

We hear stories about Baptist churches where everyone believes in total immersion for baptism, and then they split by simply moving a piano from one side of the auditorium to the other. But let's not get proud.

Old-time Methodists used to agree that total abstinence from alcoholic beverages was necessary. Then people would leave a church because the pastor didn't say hello often enough. Yes, there's lots more.

It takes tolerance to get along as Christ would have us get along. Whether it's worship or something else, we are all God's children.

I like to think of Christians as being like a beautiful, many-colored rainbow. Let's shout the praises of our God or let's kneel in a sanctuary in complete silence.

Isn't God good to us? Like children, we go through our lives working out our salvation in fear and trembling. When we arrive at our real home, He will dry our tears and say, "Welcome."

68

The Whole-Hearted Support of Wife in Ministry Makes a Monumental Difference

"**H**e has the call," she said confidently and proudly. Well, the young lady was his wife and she was talking about the ministry. It was a moment with a glow to it.

The young man knew she had revealed what he had experienced. God had called him to be a minister and he must act on that. There was happiness and seriousness.

Her words were spoken before their fathers, mothers, brothers, and sisters. It was a time of leaning on God as never before.

While he was a strong and talented person, his wife's whole-hearted support would make a very big difference. She knew there would be frustrations and disappointments.

She was already determined to go with him and minister with him in joys and sorrows. It was an inspirational scene. They loved one another and their beautiful children.

Of course, it was all important that he had the call. Otherwise, no announcement would have been made. The ministry is not for those who see it simply as another job.

So they began their lives, in a way, for the second time. Nothing would ever be the same again. To be sure, it was dramatic and emotionally exhausting.

What they had solidly on their side was the call and her support. Such support in the years to come would make the difference between success and failure.

My heart goes out to those who will walk this road together. There will be days in the future that all they will have is one another. Even church people can be cruel.

They will live in a so-called fish bowl for years to come. Some parishioners will walk the second mile with them. Others will plot and plan their departure.

While those of us who have been in the ministry a long time need your prayers, the young couples really need them. Temptation will come from totally unexpected sources.

Seemingly minor things can become major in a single day. Satan will probe and manipulate in more ways than they can imagine. It is not an easy life.

Praises be to God that the call was unquestioned and her support was a gem for all to see. Under God the future belongs to them. Some will stand in awe before this ministry.

69   A Community in Need of God's Healing Touch

"**W**e need a win-win situation," the school superintendent said forcefully. Things had gotten out of hand. Parents, students, teachers, and administrators were all in an uproar.

Reason seemed to take some days off and good people were throwing stones at one another. There were lacerations and cuts all over the place. The community suffered.

Who would be fired and who would get to stay? The differences in opinion were growing to a dangerous point that meant someone must lose and someone must win.

This was not at all a promising thing for the school system or the community. The superintendent had the answer but would people cooperate? Tension mounted.

Things had become so drastic that it looked like hurt upon hurt would go on indefinitely. There might not be any winners.

The superintendent was a fine man and known for his caring and expertise. He gave himself unselfishly to the task of pulling things together. Sleepless nights and disrespect from others filled his life.

Of course, all of this took its toll and after some months he was diagnosed with cancer. This left things mostly in the hands of others. The fighting continued.

His pastor called on him regularly and they became quite close friends. The dear Lord was always present during their sharing. It was a precious but unwanted opportunity.

Some wondered if the community could ever be put back together again. It was as though the devil was loose and would not be denied his evil deeds. What could anyone do?

The health of their leader continually worsened. Even though he was only in his fifties, the death angel was approaching. Some were concerned about his plight and others could care less.

The pastor was called to his bedside and the two had their last visit in this world. The power of the Holy Spirit abided and provided. They took turns smiling and weeping.

Several hours later the pastor was called to be with the superintendent's widow. They both stood at the man's bed and gazed in great appreciation on his face. He was at peace for the first time in months.

The funeral was in his church. The pastor preached his heart out and pleaded with God that the community might be healed. There were those who understood that he had laid down his life for their community.

70 A New Beginning

"**A** new beginning is what I desperately need." She was in her mid-forties and their divorce had been finalized only a few days before. It had been almost painless and some thought unnecessary.

She and her husband had been married more than twenty years. Their youngest child had finished high school. The other two were making it in the world, mostly with successes.

Her husband hadn't really found another woman. She certainly had not found another man. Both had found others attractive but that was about as far as it went.

What happened was a subtle and sinister growing apart. As the years passed, they hardly spoke to one another for days at a time. Both had their careers and that seemed enough.

She was an elementary school teacher and a good one. He was a pharmacist and well respected. Their combined income was more than adequate and provided college assistance for their children.

One day they woke up and said almost simultaneously that their marriage wasn't important. For them it was the dawning of a certain reality. But it was very sad.

The sadness was especially at the point of lack of spiritual interest. Churches and that kind of thing didn't mean much to them. The country club and a couple of service clubs were satisfying.

She initially began to think of a new beginning in the context of more schooling and different organizations. The spiritual side of things was absent. Who needed that sort of thing?

Fortunately, God would not leave her alone and some of her friends refused to stop praying. In time, she began to understand her life in a new way. Others sighed in relief.

She began to do more than read a prayer now and then. Holy Scripture seemed to come alive. Soon she cried—even wept—about her divorce, and saw it in a new light.

Her husband and marriage meant a lot more to her than she had realized. The divorce should never have happened, but it did. That meant she lived with the fallout, but not gracefully.

Little did she know that her ex-husband was going through a similar process. He, too, wondered why on earth their marriage had been dissolved. He also began to shed tears.

God's will and the ongoing prayers of people brought them back together. They were reunited in a private ceremony. Indeed, what God has joined together, let not man put asunder.

71   Children Can Fall Victim to Mental Harassment

"I know what you are thinking," she told her son. He was eight years old and very intimidated by his mother's words. They had a way of depressing him, according to his father.

Was it a control mechanism or just an innocent mother's way of gently relating to her son? Whatever it was, it influenced him as he was growing up.

By the time he was a teenager, he had begun to cope with the words in his own way. It became a game to see if she really knew his thoughts and to what extent.

It was like playing cat and mouse. Her son kept attempting to avoid anything and everything that seemed to show what he was thinking. Lying became commonplace.

Dad watched almost helplessly as mother and son seemed to spend their time moving around on a chessboard. When would one of them crack or one of them submit to the other?

As the young man approached high school graduation and his eighteenth birthday, he was deeply troubled. Was there nothing she thought she didn't know about him?

The problem had emerged as something deeply psychological and spiritual. He had begun to wonder if his soul belonged to him or his mother. Did God have anything to say about this?

Some people closest to him thought he went to college with a fragmented personality. In her own way, she still reminded him she knew his thoughts because, after all, she was his mother.

The father became very concerned. It was as though mother and son were locked in a power struggle. Son had learned to play the game and desperately tried to free himself.

By now he could hear her words, even though she was nowhere near. The tapes in his head seemed to roll, regardless of where he was or what he was doing. Sad.

Finally, he began to work with both a trusted pastor and psychiatrist. His inability to free himself from her domination had taken a terrible toll. He was hospitalized.

The mother died in a car accident. Now, she was physically gone and could no longer say she knew his thoughts. This did not prove therapeutic for him. In fact, he felt guilty.

The young man eventually improved and was able to sense his own freedom and worth as a human being. Mothers and fathers, it is absolutely necessary our children grow up and become their own persons.

72   A Short Course in Basic Economics 101

"Save up for a rainy day," a good father said to his son. Grandfather had the same philosophy. Son wasn't much interested in whether it rained or shined, was hot or cold.

Whoever heard tell of a rainy day, especially as it pertained to money? Both Dad and Grandfather had ample means. Even if he couldn't pay the bills he created, someone would.

The young man either couldn't or wouldn't understand the need for money beyond the moment. There would always be someone to come up with it. There was no need to get uptight about such things.

His understanding of life in a financial sense was really quite simple. If he couldn't come up with necessary funds, someone else would. It always seemed to work out that way.

Well, after two years of college, he found himself dead broke. Loans, scholarships, and his part-time income all dried up about the same time. It would take two more years to get his degree.

Surely, either Dad or Grandfather had just the right amount to see him through. Much to his surprise, they did not budge. He felt betrayed and couldn't believe them.

Why wouldn't they write the checks? He asked them as humbly as he could, but with a ring of disgust in his voice. About then, he was given the opportunity to grow up quickly.

They both came at him the same way. They wondered why he hadn't paid attention to the rainy day idea. Were they so old-fashioned they rated no consideration? Gloomy reality descended.

When he made excuses, he learned they knew a lot more about how he spent his money than he had realized. In fact, they shamed him by pointing out that he wasted the money from his part-time job.

He thought to himself that since he made it, he had the right to spend it as he darn well pleased. Fortunately, he didn't say that openly and saved himself from a heated sermon.

The more the two older men talked, the more he began to capture a glimpse of life as it truly is. They had lived a lot longer than he had. Their wisdom was grudgingly accepted.

His money had dried up. Since his pride was largely gone, he pleaded for twenty dollars to take his girlfriend out for the evening. Father and Grandfather came up with ten dollars each.

For the moment his countenance changed. Then, in almost the same voice, they told him the loan had to be paid back in ten days. Now, he had the opportunity to pass Basic Economics 101.

"I'm going shopping," Mom said, in tones that she expected a delightful afternoon. There was that lilt in her voice. Something really good was going to come out of this trip.

Her teenage daughter told her good-bye and settled in to watch the soaps on television. As she watched, certain assumptions began to build. Mom's trip would be useful. The daughter began to have these wonderful assumptions. All of them were directed towards her mother's trip. Wow, what promise.

After all, they had talked for days about things teenagers needed. The list was not long and Mom would deliver. She began to look forward to her mother's return.

Mom came home just in time to fix a six-o'clock dinner. She had a couple of packages. They weren't all that big but that didn't matter because she assumed the small things were for her.

Well, first of all, she asked her mother about her favorite cosmetic line. Mom didn't seem all that interested and indicated she hadn't brought anything like that home.

Next, her daughter inquired about a T-shirt that everyone had but her. Surely that was in one of the packages. Her mother quickly pointed out that was not among her purchases.

Then came the big assumption. She told her mom how they had visited at length about this new, best-selling novel. It was the one that would aid her in one of her classes.

Once again, Mom just did not deliver the goods. In fact, Mom had bought a couple of paperbacks just for herself. They weren't even remotely on her daughter's list.

Even though the assumptions were built on past experience and relationships, they were all false. Not one of them panned out. Daughter batted a big zero and gloom entered.

You and I have a lot of assumptions, don't we? This is not all bad. However, unless they are built upon doing good for others, maybe we *should* be disappointed. We must take another look.

What is it right now that you know is going to come true? How big are your assumptions? When you discover you are wrong, then what is going to happen?

Please talk to God about this sometimes painful state of affairs. He will grant you clear vision. He will give you a new perspective that gets rid of me, my, and mine.

74   Being Formed into a Good Man

"Lovely, simply lovely," the well-dressed and gracious lady said. Those who had observed her over the years wondered about these words. It seemed like at every social occasion they were the same.

When she saw another woman whose attire was attractive, she would use the same words. When she heard a man speak of a current success, again they were the same. The list could get very long.

Let's don't be too hard on her because, frankly, we do the same thing. For many of us the words are "nice" or "good." What or who is a nice person anyway? The same is true for a good person.

I happen to believe there is a way out of this for those of us especially spiritually oriented. This is true as we talk about a good man. Recall what the army officer said at the Crucifixion.

Just after Jesus had commended His spirit to God, the officer exclaimed, "Certainly, he was a good man." Now, we are onto something. No longer do we have to wonder nearly as much.

For me, being a genuinely good man means you have undergone a conversion experience. Maybe it was instantaneous or perhaps a two-year confirmation class. Whatever, it must be legitimate.

Yes, and a genuinely good man is one of prayer. He gets up praying and he goes to bed praying. In a way, his entire life is one of prayer as he goes about daily activities.

Then, I firmly believe he is a man immersed in the Holy Scriptures. Over the years, under the guidance of the Holy Spirit, he has been formed by them. They are part of his flesh and blood.

I also understand a genuine good man knows that faith and works go together. They are intended to be two sides of the same coin. You have faith; then show me your good works and vice versa.

Yes, and how can you leave out the expression of your faith and works or witnessing? The best kind is that which is so spontaneous and natural it never calls attention to what's happening.

Isn't the aim of life and death being formed spiritually in the image of Christ and the apostles? Saint Paul says whether I live or die, I belong to Christ. How wonderful it is.

So, words we toss around rather aimlessly can have real meaning. Perhaps that's not correct all the time. However, we do have a handle on that which is genuinely good.

I don't know about you, but I want to die a genuinely good man. For me, that is the highest and best form of success there is. If you haven't done so, come and join me today.

75   Retired, But Not From God's Army

"I'm retired but not tired," he said pointedly and with feeling. He had passed sixty-five and it was time to hang it up. Well over thirty-five years with his employer was enough.

The celebrations were appropriate and with appreciation for his good work. His wife had mixed feelings. She was glad he would be at home more, but what was she going to do with him?

Their children were exuberant in praise for their parents. At last, maybe they could do the kinds of things they never had time to do. They had worked hard.

Yet, no one could miss the emphasis in Dad's direct statement. Truth of the matter was, he wasn't quite ready to retire. So, a lingering unrest had begun in his soul.

It wasn't that he had been treated unfairly. He had his share of respect, and the longevity with one company in some ways was remarkable. A good thing had happened.

So, the days and weeks passed. Before long, a whole year had come and gone. The unrest had begun to diminish and he—along with his wife—were beginning to enjoy themselves.

They were religious people and thanked God for the new dimension in their lives. He couldn't believe some of his habits had begun to be altered. Things had become downright pleasant.

Then, it happened. God had work for him to do. He was a good speaker, enjoyed people, had a flair for promotion, and knew a great deal about administration.

His pastor and the area committee on the ministry wanted him to do the necessary things, leading up to pastoring a small church. It was a shock and he equivocated.

Had God called or did some ministers just think he should be with a difficult, little, and floundering church? He had made a solid transition into retirement.

Then, the Holy Spirit began to remind him than even though retired, he was not tired. He was humbled and remembered vividly what he had said. Soon, there would be no more Sundays off.

His wife wasn't all that enthusiastic. However, she recognized the situation and could sense the Lord was calling. It would be a terrible thing to disobey the living God.

After a year or so, he became a licensed preacher. As you might guess, a small church was available and waiting. Sometimes our God's ways are not all that mysterious.

76   "The Battle Hymn of the Republic" Stirs the Patriotic Heartstrings

"Oh, please keep singing," the lady pleaded. She was in tears and the patriotic fervor with joy was in her happy face.

It was the Fourth of July and the moment was precious. The congregation was singing one of those few songs that can move us into supernatural joy and strength. Electricity was in the air. It was as though they had been lifted to heavenly heights.

The song was "The Battle Hymn of the Republic," written by Julia Ward Howe. Frankly, folks, there really isn't anything like it for many of us. Its spiritual power is awesome.

"Mine eyes have seen the glory of the coming of the Lord" calls to something very deep within us. Those words are filled with confidence and a sense of the Ultimate in our midst.

Some years ago at First United Methodist Church in Seymour, I invited a singing group to come on a Sunday evening for a patriotic presentation. For an hour and a half, they were really inspirational.

Then came the closing number. You guessed it. It was "The Battle Hymn of the Republic," and dozens upon dozens sang their hearts out in a magnificent display of patriotism.

Upon leaving, one old codger—usually very unemotional—said to me, with big tears streaming down his cheeks, an insightful thing. He had made up his mind he wouldn't leave until they sang it.

He had waited all evening and he didn't care much what else they did. This song moved him more than any other. Friends, that's not the first time or the last time I have heard that.

The refrain is like singing from Holy Scripture. "Glory, glory, hallelujah. His truth is marching on." It concludes and we know we shall never be completely defeated.

What a privileged people Americans are. We can never say "thank you" enough for this truly great nation. World history says no one has ever seen a nation like it.

Our songs are a big help in expressing the sheer honor of being a part of this land and its history. Real problems have come and gone. New ones beckon to be solved.

Lift up your heads and shout into the heavens with thanksgiving the providential care of the God of the entire universe. It is hard to find all the words we deeply feel.

Indeed, "In the beauty of the lilies Christ was born across the sea, with a glory in his bosom that transfigures you and me." Today the Crucified and Resurrected Christ lives among us.

77 Whatever You Do, There Are Possibilities

"He had the hide of an alligator," said the young fellow, who was speaking of his grandfather. The comment was not derogatory. In fact, it was quite complimentary.

The comment was made at the old man's funeral. He was eighty at death and seemed to be just as tough as he was at fifty or sixty. This was the consensus of those who knew him.

Of course, the grandson had a much closer look and marveled at how tough he really was. No one was made that strong and durable today. His grandfather was a different breed.

Grandson learned to fish and hunt from him. Often he wanted to quit and go home to watch TV or just hang out. Grandfather would have none of that.

Lakes and streams all had lots of possibilities for catching fish of various sizes. Forests and meadows were always good for rabbits and whatever else moved about.

It took some time and several outings before Grandson learned a principle of life that is always essential to success. Whatever you do, there are always possibilities.

Extended, that means every situation provides us with the chance to make use of the moment. We can better ourselves and hopefully many, many others.

When you stick with something long enough, a positive action or reaction occurs. We have to forget about the inconveniences, yes, and the scratches and bruises.

It amazed the young fellow how Grandfather could still be tough, really tough, up until the very day he died. There was also a lesson in that.

As long as we are alive, possibilities are present. Think of the successful careers that have started after sixty-five and even older. God has given all of us remarkable chances to succeed.

When I was sixty-six, the bishop appointed me to Yorktown United Methodist Church. It had marvelous property and a strategic location. Most of all it had quality, spiritually minded people.

So, for four years, I labored in a wonderful vineyard. In some ways, I accomplished more there than any other appointment. Mind you, this was after the usual time of retirement.

In reflection, this was God's way of showing me that as long as I am alive and willing, the possibilities for real success will be there. It is cause for daily thanksgiving.

"Don't cram that down my throat," he said in words and feelings no one could misunderstand. He was fuming and had enough of what he was hearing. In fact, more than enough.

The salesman, a slick and crafty fellow, had stepped over the line. He had pushed too hard and the backlash was obvious to all in the vicinity. The salesman had misjudged his quarry.

What do you suppose the problem was? Was the man doing the selling a liar? Perhaps it was a case of quoting so-called facts that weren't facts at all along with an arrogant approach.

In a nutshell, the man's intelligence had been insulted. Mr. Salesman treated him like someone who had little or no education and limited experience. In a way, the result could be predicted.

Believe it or not, I have seen this happen in churches. Not always, but most often, the pastor is the guilty one. He or she treats laity in such a way they are demeaned over and over.

Just about the worst thing a pastor can do is insult the intelligence of lay persons.

I have believed for many years the only way to pastor a church successfully is to do so in a collegial fashion. Key leaders, especially, must be treated as valued parishioners.

A pastor may be very well-educated and skilled but lack a sense of equal importance so necessary in the parish. Share your leadership with them. This within itself is a growth experience.

In my travels, sparks fly between pastor and people whenever a pastor superimposes his will on those whose intelligence may exceed his or hers. Don't insult those you are supposed to lead.

While the office of pastor is one of power, it must never be used as a put down. The buck may stop there, but that's no excuse to put laity in their place. Servanthood is an absolute necessity.

Granted some heads are hard and threats come in many forms. My experience is that laity who become overbearing are usually controlled by other laity. Pastors, pay attention.

Pastors prove themselves best and pay their dues most fittingly by Christlike gentleness that is supported by ongoing faithfulness. Faithfulness always includes humility and sincerity.

So, pastors never insult the intelligence of your laity. In many ways, most of them are smarter than you are. So, underline loving patience and the power of the Cross.

79   A Hearty Combination: Wisdom, Courage, Sensitivity

"**C**all it what you like," Dad bemoaned. He was a shrewd fellow who sometimes made people feel very uncomfortable by his wisdom. Others would testify he was seldom wrong.

Really it was a combination of wisdom, courage, and sensitivity. Sooner or later people learned not to try to pull one over on him. He could see through insincerity quickly and thoroughly.

Perhaps the greatest gift he had was to perceive the way language was used and misused. He was always asking what this title meant and what that one meant.

He was good. He could take a highfalutin' title or label and reduce it to bare bones, leaving the holder virtually naked with embarrassment. He was almost an entertainer.

It takes people like that in our world to keep us honest. Dad was giving a very practical gift to his children. He especially wanted them to see that glitter and glow can be empty.

Questionable public relations persons have long used exaggeration with the clever manipulation of words. They often sell anyone or anything. If we are alert, we see it every day we live.

The quality of someone can seldom be determined by titles and labels. You can see this in all professions. Doctor So-and-so may be highly esteemed, but his or her doctorate may be from a degree mill.

It's a lot like never judging a book by its cover. Book jackets can make you believe you are buying brilliance par excellence. Reading it will change your life tremendously for the good.

Isn't it interesting—Bibles almost never come highly recommended? Oh, there are some exceptions. However, the quality of the Scriptures recommend themselves directly and simply.

We need more dads and moms like we have mentioned. In today's world the hype given birth by clever and misleading words can seriously jeopardize the future of young people.

Now, we could make an exception among some clergy. The honorary doctor of divinity degree might very well be given for years of service. It can reflect excellent ministry over a long period.

Frankly, I prefer my doctor of ministry degree that requires several months of academic and practical labor. It taught me to look carefully for quality, especially in the area of preaching.

Join me, if you will, in helping one another to get beyond titles and labels. Strange as it may sound, our very souls could be at stake. High potentate really might mean low integrity.

80   A Tribute to the Memory of Bud McCall

"**I** wish I had known him better," an acquaintance lamented. Death had come to a prominent and respected figure. He wished he had known the man in a more complete way.

Like so many of us, it seemed the time was never right or he needed to do this or that. While biographical sketches might be of help, flesh and blood contact was gone.

Yes, I suppose everyone who has lived well into adulthood has had this experience. It is somewhat exasperating. Time has run out for them and for us as well.

I wished I had known "Bud" McCall better. He and my father were first cousins. I guess that made us second cousins. At any rate, you get the picture and I am proud of it.

While I was traveling about the state serving United Methodist churches, Bud was staying put tending his vineyard. He loved his family, New Castle, and Henry County.

I learned he was a practitioner of the power of practical politics. Not much escaped him. Fortunately, I was able to be at his home before his passing, visiting with him and his lovely wife.

The man was a genius at the local level. He gave himself in so many different ways. When the county hurt, he hurt. He could laugh or cry with his people, maybe the same day.

It is an enriching experience to travel about, especially in the churches. Yet, I sometimes wonder if Bud didn't have the right idea all along. Contributions are made by staying put.

We live in an age of travel and continually changing environments. Our children and grandchildren have already seen more places and people than we will ever see.

Maybe there is someone you admire at a distance and have not fully become acquainted. Take steps to remedy that. If you will take the initiative, my guess is you will be surprised by the outcome.

God places in our midst many interesting and helpful people. By the way, all persons are interesting. All you have to do is take the time and energy to be around them and be non-judgmental.

In politics people especially count. Elections can be won or lost by the vote of just a few of them. Whenever you don't take them seriously, most likely your political career is over and should be.

But back to Bud. He is the only person I have ever known who had two of Indiana's Sagamore of the Wabash honors, one from Governor Bayh and the other from Governor O'Bannon. I don't even have one and, frankly, I am a bit jealous.

81   Seven Steps to Relieve Stress

"Let me alone," she said bluntly and without hesitation. In short, she did not want to be bothered. Anyone who sought to relate to her at that moment was at risk.

Those of us in public life or in situations of stress, I dare say, have all blurted out that request. We need a chance to recuperate. We can't get it done by people pressing upon us.

Even the most extroverted men and women have a need to back away for a quiet time. The replenishing of energy and an attitude adjustment result. It's nature's way for all of us.

Each of us has a right to his or her privacy. This is God-given and no one has the right to take it away from us. In a way, it is also a constitutional right, conferred upon us as Americans.

Beyond generalities, what does being let alone add up to in a positive sense? Obviously, our experiences are unique, but I believe certain things are very helpful and even needful.

First, there is the clearing away of excessive stimuli that keeps us on the go. Hit the stop button and sigh in relief that you don't have to do or say something clever. That system is closed.

Second, pause for a time and allow no interference in your peacefulness. Celebrate the moment. You might even want to proclaim, "Thank you, Jesus," several times.

Third, begin to reflect on all the strands of your life of which you are aware. Try not to miss something that is significant but don't press yourself. Tiptoe away from anxiety.

Fourth, settle in on those who have given you so much. Please don't allow money to become a major factor. Also, please shy away from those who think you owe them something.

Fifth, ponder the times you know God has been in full control of your life. Thank Him for the times He took care of you in spite of your shenanigans. Ask Him to forgive you.

Sixth, ask yourself about what tomorrow brings. Do not worry about it. Plead in confidence for God's providence and provision but do not attempt to direct His will.

Seventh, tell yourself over and over that God loves you and it is because He says so through His Son, Jesus the Christ. Please don't hurry. Allow tears of joy to flood your entire being.

All seven steps are significant. There is no specific time schedule for any of this process and every person should feel rejuvenated. Now enter the world of human action again.

82   Envy, Revenge Tarnish a Good Reputation

"The vultures are gathering," his father said with seriousness. Father knew the setting and the conditions. He was concerned and yet resigned to the reality of what was happening.

His son was a very successful physician in the community. In fact, his reputation was statewide and beyond. His name meant professional expertise and integrity, plus a spotless private life.

You can imagine the latent envy that existed among a few less-than-successful people. They got their chance, or should we say, they *created* it.

Something questionable emerged. Among a team of doctors, a mistake was made. While no one died, someone didn't receive the best of care.

Soon everything seemed to gravitate to his son and lack of know-how.

The father could see it all unfolding before his very eyes. Indeed, the vultures had been waiting and now they were openly gathering. Would they eventually be able to feed from his carcass?

Life is a lot like that, isn't it? A good name and genuine success are two things most people want. To see someone else have this, over a period of time, brings out the worst in some people.

On the lighter side, I heard a pastor say something humorously profound and pertinent. He said after he became successful, he didn't know he had dated so many girls that he had never met. That's life, too.

But back to this dear man's physician son. Little by little, his name and reputation began to be tarnished. I believe the father's heart ached more than the son's, and sadness engulfed him.

In time, just short of litigations, things began to turn around. The vultures were beginning to disperse. For the first time in weeks, hope came on the scene, beautiful and promising.

What happened? The community organized itself and began to deal in facts and confronted a jealous spin factory. Many prominent citizens decided this was not going to happen to such a fine man.

It took months of persistent community pressure to put things back in place. Perhaps the most persuasive tool was the numerous patients who had been treated by the physician.

Isn't it strange how years of near-perfect practice can almost be canceled by one questionable event? Yes, that's life, also. May God be merciful if you are drawn into that kind of destruction.

The father's heart mended before he died. His son kept on being genuinely successful and more than 90 percent of the community was joyous. Dear friends, not all such stories end that well.

"It was not to be," she said in sorrowful tones. A son was dealing with serious illness; in fact it was multiple sclerosis. The best medical care was received and prayers were said by many.

After some months, his nervous system was seriously diminished in effectiveness. Speech defects and loss of muscular coordination were persisting. His mother gave up.

When mothers bring their children into the world, they must have high hopes for them. In my experience, I believe this is especially true in terms of health. Disappointment sometimes comes.

In this case, the mother was mostly fatalistic, resigning herself to what was not to be. We can quarrel with this attitude. Of course, we are not in her shoes and that makes a lot of difference.

Some might even suggest she and her church did not pray long enough and hard enough. In short, if they had stayed on their knees long enough, God would have granted a miracle.

To my way of thinking, this is cruel and really accomplishes nothing positive. It seems like attempting to force God into doing something He is not going to do. What a terrible guilt trip.

Sometimes we view and experience life in such a way that for us there is only one acceptable answer. In our current situation, surely a merciful God would intercede.

Frankly, I have never been much of a believer in fate. Yet, there is this lingering thought that God in His providence has plans we cannot change. Even good living and prayer are to no avail.

Is this very negative? I really don't think that is the case. We can succumb to an unnecessary attitude of God's lack of concern. It helps greatly to remember God is God.

In my college years, I was deeply smitten by understanding life in a predestinarian fashion. In short, the Creator had decided things in advance. There wasn't much I could do.

We have begun to travel in some deep and complicated areas. Don't give up; please stay with me. There is no reason to back away and buy into a negative fatalism.

The mother's son's life and death seemed set in cement. He had never done anything to deserve this and was quite an exemplary young fellow. All of this appeared to be so unfair.

The truth is he died after a few years and his condition had only worsened. However, his family and friends never abandoned him. His gift: he taught them much about coping, compassion, and kindness.

84   Learning to Forgive Yourself Is a Must

"It was an honest mistake," he told his wife. She seemed to have pulled a really big blooper and was severely depressed. In fact, it had become hard for her to leave the house.

As gently and sometimes firmly as he could, he kept saying, "It was an honest mistake." Her husband was at a loss for words and almost ready to give up. He didn't stop praying and hoping.

She had virtually gone through a personality change. Most of her married life she had been so outgoing and vivacious. The community knew her as an asset to her family and others.

Briefly, she had made a mistake about a slate of officers in her sorority. When she gave the report to the full membership, she had the wrong name for the new treasurer.

When asked about it, she became defensive and argued, finally in a loud voice. It was a most disconcerting scene. Finally, the minutes of the nominating committee were read.

It was evident to everyone present she was mistaken. Embarrassment and pain began. In fact, she was humiliated in her eyes and that began to be the real problem.

She had become inactive and very withdrawn. Her sisters had invited her back for a time and attempted to soothe her feelings. Now they, more or less, stayed their distance.

Bless her heart. She just couldn't forgive herself, even though she intended nothing harmful to anyone. Over and over the tapes were playing in her head, *How could you be so stupid?*

It got so bad some days that her thinking bordered on being incoherent. She recognized the danger and fortunately sought guidance in the Holy Scriptures. Healing was about to begin.

In 1 Thessalonians 5:16, she ran across these words: "Be joyful always, pray at all times, be thankful in all circumstances." She quickly noted those words did not resemble her life at all.

A day or so later, Proverbs 3:5 said, "Trust in the Lord with all your heart. Never rely on what you think you know." A vengeful and prideful self became crystal clear.

Now she was shedding tears of relief and recovery, instead of dejection and deprecation. It had become almost solely her problem and she had perpetuated a mistake honestly made.

Days became better and the nights were filled with sleep. Everyone greeted her months later at the next annual gathering. It may have been the best meeting the ladies ever had.

85   "Set-Up" for a Hidden Agenda

"Thanks, but no thanks," a gentleman related in a tone you couldn't miss. Someone was offering a gift that had obvious strings to it. He appreciated the offer but did not want to get involved.

Ingratitude is such a frightening sight. Yet, we do have to be careful, don't we? The best way to handle those people who want to be helpful but who have a hidden agenda is like this gentleman.

If we can keep from it, we never should hurt other people's feelings. Of course, if their feelings are hurt by an intended "set-up"—deliberate manipulation—they have conjured up, that's too bad. We are to be people of integrity, especially Christians.

Those of us in public life over the years are faced with these situations much more than we would like. It is not always easy to provide a win-win experience. "No thanks" must be underlined.

In the maze and myriad of human encounters, it is sometimes hard to know how to react. Young pastors are especially vulnerable. They want to please every parishioner and, of course, that is impossible.

While Paul said he became all things to all people in order to save some, we are not Paul. I do believe, however, we can please others in God's sight by simply obeying the Holy Spirit.

That sounds easy, doesn't it? It may be easier than you think, provided you spend enough time in a prayerful mood. Just spiritually nestle up to your Savior and Lord like a child.

The ordained ministry today must provide persons rightly related to God the Father through Jesus the Christ. This means integrity is an absolute must. We must never, never be for sale.

Laity can be of real help, but don't put your pastor in a questionable position. If you need to test him/her for a high level of integrity, why is he/she your pastor in the first place?

Pastors need to be given the benefit of the doubt, as some of us used to say. To provide a no-win situation on purpose eventually hurts the congregation and their witness to the community.

But let's not be too hasty. Sometimes pastors put laity in uncomfortable positions and those dear people are afraid to say, "Thanks, but no thanks." Shame on you, reverend.

So, folks, there is enough of that kind of thing to go around. I pray you will never be less than what God wants you to be. Games in the life of the church are hurtful, maybe sinful.

I give you a closing suggestion. If you give a gift in the expectation of something in return, don't embarrass yourself before others . . . especially your heavenly Father. Be alert, the tempter roams around.

86   The Built-In Privileges of a Grandson Come to Light

"Let's pretend," a six-year-old said joyfully to his grandmother. His eyes were dancing and whatever he wanted to do always interested her. He was her pride and joy . . . and more.

Since he was the only grandson, there were naturally special built-in privileges. If he wanted to pretend, that was what he should do. There would be no restrictions on this boy.

So, he began launching his imagination in different directions. She praised him and told how smart he was. This went on for several minutes to the delight of both.

Then, his little blue eyes seemed to glaze over, as he began visualizing things that totally amazed her. It seemed as though violence had come directly out of the TV into his full-scale expressions.

He began to shout about death and injury, unexplored planets and aliens, and men/women with awesome weapons. Worlds were colliding and the U.S. was up for grabs. Her mouth dropped open.

What on this sacred earth was going on? He was a first-grader and had good parents who loved him. Grandmother thought he might even be the most perfect child she had seen.

After a few moments, his pretending was over. But he did want to know what she thought about his trip into make-believe. In his own childlike way, he was trying to impress her.

Well, I guess parents and grandparents alike are very surprised about the little ones. Why should we be assaulted by the kinds of television shows so easily available?

Yes, children are impressionable and they always have been. Probably the big difference in generations is the control factor. Various forms of media inundate us whether we like it or not.

We can shrug our shoulders and say it's simply a passing phase that will have little to do with his development. In a few years, it will be as though nothing negative influenced him.

If we take that tack, we are kidding ourselves. Our environment always helps to mold us into what we eventually become. Hopefully, the little fellow will sift and sort as he grows up.

So much depends on what parents and grandparents do to expose children to healthy experiences. That doesn't mean being controlling. It especially means ongoing sincere prayer.

When I was his age, I collected toy guns and shot more people than I can remember. Dad thought I might become a gangster (really). But he and Mom prayed for me . . . sometimes I heard them.

87   Bring on the Easter Bunnies

"Bring on the Easter bunnies," her older brother gleefully intoned. It wouldn't be long. It was a tradition in the family to have the bunnies all around on that Sunday.

They looked forward to it and especially the older brother who had planned a virtual extravaganza for his little sister. She was barely three and he adored her. He was a good boy.

His problem and that of the family is a common one across the United States. Easter bunnies in their various forms, shapes, and often, flavors, seem to overtake us. Should we deal with it?

I have never had a quarrel with a Christian family allowing those winsome little creatures into the house. Why? I know they will be seen and appreciated in a right way.

This precious day is about—*really* about—Jesus arising from the dead. Once that is set in place and worship taken place, we view the bunnies in a different light. They are not the focus.

So, it is a matter of what (who) is first, isn't it? If children grow up believing these lovable little animals, edible or non-edible, are all there is to Easter, may God be merciful.

While the dividing line appears to be thin in such matters, I have my doubts. When we accept and worship the risen Lord, nothing else approaches His greatest victory and ours as well.

I had a lady once say to me, "But they are just children and aren't old enough to know anything about religion." That is deceptive because the little ones always watch adults.

The power of children to imitate those older around them is phenomenal. If there is no strong sense of the Resurrection in parents, I firmly believe each and every child is disadvantaged.

When children are in worship with their parents, there is a certain dynamic at work. When grace is given at the table, the same holds true. There is a long list that helps shape those little minds.

Dear friends, pray daily for those boys and girls who have never been taught in any significant way about Christ and His church. How many are there? Far too many for you and me to count.

Fathers and mothers, if Easter is all about bunnies, fall on your knees and repent. Then, arise in forgiveness and take your children to a solid Bible-believing church where the Resurrected Lord reigns.

It is a cliché, but nevertheless, children are the most precious gift we have. Yes, and let's be honest, God will not find us guiltless if we fail to show and tell them Easter's meaning.

"Son, it's all about service," a concerned father explained briefly. His son was in his early twenties and testing the waters of life. His pressing concern was looking after number one.

His father was hoping to find a way to guide and help, not interfere and dominate. Finally, something came to him that he had overlooked. Dad wondered why he hadn't thought of it before.

It had to do with belonging to a service club. There he would be exposed to men and women who were involved in service to others. There would be fun, comradeship, and some work.

Personally and professionally, one of my greatest joys has been to be part of a service club in most communities where I have served. Wherever you go, there are always those who can help.

Frankly, I have discovered Rotary clubs to be especially worthwhile. Not only is there a sense of service, there is a sense of responsibility. The good that is done shines brightly in many ways.

I believe this is especially based upon the "Four-Way Test." It amazes me how deeply religious this is in the best sense of the word. There is no sectarianism. I have never seen anyone argue over what church is best.

"Is it the truth?" is first. In all our relationships, I know of no better way to begin. If we can't deal in truth, we can't possibly expect things to go well among us.

"Is it fair to all concerned?" is second. You may say that is expecting entirely too much. But think about the way it makes your heart and mind work; then, you will discover it's power.

"Will it build good will and better friendships?" is third. That really gets down to where we live and something that most all of us desire. Look at it locally or worldwide.

"Will it be beneficial to all concerned?" is fourth. Humanity has been working at that for a long, long time. Sometimes, we pastors really struggle with this one and have to trust God for the outcome.

I have often marveled at the way a good service club can negotiate its way through problems. In humility, I must admit there are moments when churches don't seem to do as well.

By now you are probably wondering about father and son. Father was right. The young man became a member of the service club and yes, it was Rotary. The exposure to self-giving was positive.

The benefits were many and they often went to the meetings together. When the son transferred jobs and moved to another city, he simply moved his membership. Self-giving can be transforming.

89   Baby Your Mother on Mother's Day

"Oh, it's just another day," she said hurriedly. She was speaking about what we traditionally know as Mother's Day. She had two sons and two daughters, who were not spending the day with her.

Her attitude reflected the children's, who had not made all that much of her special day. She was not feeling sorry for herself. In a way, she was just conditioning herself for another ho-hum Mother's Day.

She had been a good mother, almost always generous and at times sacrificial. Her husband had been sensitive to the way she had treated their children. In fact, he was her biggest fan.

For some reason, the children just never caught on. Oh, there would be cards now and then, but they were not always on time. Rarely were there gifts and seldom flowers.

Were they forgetful or did they take her for granted?

Children, don't take your mother for granted. On Mother's Day, "baby" her. Yes, that is what I said and meant it.

You only have one. She may not be perfect, but I certainly don't know any perfect children. Heap up the cards and gifts and if need be, rent a U–Haul to bring them to her door.

Oh yes, mothers should never cook on this day. It is hurtful to their health (well, not really). Take her to the best place around and buy her something delicious, leaving a big tip.

By now some of you may be thinking he is trying to send us on a guilt trip or just flat-out exaggerating. I guess if the shoe fits, you should wear it and I am not exaggerating.

I have known some children who have lavished expensive gifts on their mothers after they were dead. That can never be a substitute for doing something truly wonderful while she is living.

Does all this sound a bit radical? I certainly hope not. It seems to me it puts in perspective a truth that contemporary society either avoids or seeks to replace in countless ways.

If you don't have enough money to spoil her, go borrow enough to give her a really wonderful day. It may very well be the best investment you have ever made. The returns are colossal.

My mother has been gone for more than ten years, and I should have done more for her. Funny how tombstones, as cold as they appear, can make you cry tears of appreciation. Best of all, God is watching.

90 Fatherhood Can Be an Awesome Power

"**I** didn't mean it," he cried out. His voice was filled with powerful emotion and concern. Not only was he serious, he was totally serious in a way that not only surprised others but him as well.

He had paddled his boy, barely three years old, until the precious little fellow was so scared he could no longer cry. Two older children and the mother were witnesses. They were quiet and sorrowful.

When Dad came to his senses, he wanted to run as far as he could and hide. Fortunately, he didn't. The little family needed to hear what he had to say and furthermore a look into his heart.

He had done a terrible thing, thinking he was teaching his son a lesson. How else could a child learn obedience? Physical punishment, after a time of disobedience, was the only way to go.

What the father didn't understand at first was the great harm in overreaction to his son's behavior. Father was on the right track but realized too late his discipline had run amuck.

But let's don't be too quick to write off this painful event. Had he not lost control, the other family members would never have seen another side of him. He was big enough to make amends.

Not only did he apologize in tears, he told them how wrong he was, and would they please forgive him? They had never seen him so humbled and distraught with guilt.

Fatherhood can be an awesome power in today's world, just like any other time. We know from reputable studies it is a necessity for family life to be fulfilled, that is, if it is a certain healthy kind.

So many fathers I have known are not bad men at all but they are often confused about their roles. Sometimes I believe we just don't grow men big enough to be healthy fathers.

Frankly, some have given up because they know whatever they do will not be enough and they are certain to be criticized. They seem to tuck their tails and fade into the background.

I am convinced much of our unrest in home is due to fathers who have not taken their Heavenly Father seriously. They have not seen their manhood closely connected to God the Father.

To be sure, this is not a new problem. Witness the generations of men who knew what was right but failed to do it. Sometimes they were afraid; often the big fear was losing their children in divorce.

Surely, we don't have to be caught in the extremes of over-reaction and lack of action. The key is found in fathers talking to their Father in Heaven, who wants them to be the best fathers they can be.

91   Grandfatherly Advice Is a Treasure

"What do you mean, you can't?" the old man bellowed. In his grandfatherly way he was about to make a powerful point with his granddaughter.

She was in her third year of college and doing well. They had always had a good relationship. From the time she was born, his favors were obvious. He delighted in her as a little girl and now a big one.

She made the good mistake of coming to him in a huff, citing the inequities of society. She paraded a long list of things and vocations closed to her because of being a woman.

After the list had been completed, he rubbed his bushy eyebrows. Silence began to pervade the moment. Finally, it was time to respond and graciousness would carry the day.

He began by saying her grandmother in some ways definitely had some limitations placed on her. In that day and time there was a subtle and not so subtle way of control.

Then he elaborated on the sheer goodness of his wife. Her self-lessness and natural skills were emphasized. She was immersed in the lives of her children and grandchildren.

In fact, he even suggested that Grandmother would probably know more about life than she ever would. Well, that was a sour note and cause for some real discomfort for both.

Soon after Grandfather finished the introduction to his sermon, he began to point out all that was available to her. She was utterly amazed about how much he knew about the world.

He had his list of everything she could be and underlined the names of a few men who would help get her there. She began to ask herself where did her grandfather get all of this.

As he moved through the main points of his sermon, he softly reiterated, "What do you mean, you can't?" He hadn't preached that well for years, and he didn't even have a license.

Now, it was time for the summary and conclusion. It was all positive and perhaps the best pep talk he had ever given. He closed by looking into her beautiful face and saying, "Of course, you can."

She kissed him on the forehead and told him how much she loved him. Then she smiled confidently and admitted that, at least, he did have something to say. It was a classic moment.

After she had gone, the old fellow mused in solitude. It was a conversation they both needed. The future was brighter for both and there was a feeling in the air that God had been present.

92   When Shepherds Cannot Get Along, the Sheep Get Confused

"The funeral was inspiring," a loved one reported with deep appreciation. The two pastors had handled it well. The funeral directors were caring and professional in every way.

Only a very small number of people knew what had happened behind the scenes. It mostly involved the two clergymen. It was a situation all of us in the ordained ministry face occasionally.

To be diplomatic, part of the family wanted one pastor to do the funeral and the other part wanted someone else. What were they to do and how could they discreetly handle this?

To be less diplomatic, the pastors really didn't like one another all that well. Both thought the other was stealing sheep. They accused one another of trying to get members to belong elsewhere.

It was widely known the two churches were very competitive, mostly in a healthy way. What was not known was the pastors' disdain for each other. God must have been greatly embarrassed.

Who would have the funeral? The family and mortuary did their planning carefully. Then, a decision had to be made; it involved some very down-to-earth and open conversation.

They decided to invite both to have the service. Fortunately, only a couple of the family members knew the depth of the problem. Both men accepted and that was the easy part, but now for the next step.

Were they willing to sit down and plan the service together or would there need to be virtually two services? They agreed to have coffee together. After the forced congeniality, something happened.

They looked at one another straight in the eyes and simultaneously said, "May God be merciful to us." Then, their eyes began to look deeply into their coffee cups as they regained composure.

Could they do that service together, honoring both the deceased and grieving family? The answer was a resounding "Yes." Our dear Lord's cross became lighter.

So, they closed ranks as pastors in the community and provided a funeral service that was indeed inspiring. God was glorified and loved ones celebrated the passing of a very important person.

Do these things really happen? Well, yes, they do and upon occasion can be far less than what is expected by gentlemen of the clergy. But give thanks. My experience is that the grace of God is working.

When shepherds cannot get along, the sheep get confused and scattered. However, God does not forsake us. In fact, through repentance and forgiveness former divisive clergy can love one another.

93 The Fishing Experience
More Than Just Fish

"The fishing was wonderful," the lad said joyfully and enthusiastically to his mother. She soon became perplexed. The reason: her son was not bragging about all the fish he had caught.

All she could find out was that it was wonderful. After he had gone to baseball practice, she sat down for her usual cold drink and began to think about the excursion. Why was it wonderful?

What did his father and grandfather have to do with this? All three of them were together at a neighbor's pond, known for its excellent fishing. They were not talking much.

What was this all about anyway? She tried to probe into her husband's mind with little success. Grandfather was even more tight-lipped, but he did smile a lot and acted happy.

Little by little, the truth came out. Her fourteen-year-old son had his first real girlfriend and what he knew about girls would fill a tiny thimble. The mystery was beginning to unravel.

While the three fishing poles were supposedly doing their work, the young fellow began to drop a few hints to Dad and Grandpa. In short, he needed to know more about girls. They were not surprised.

So, the three-hour venture was mostly about—you guessed it—girls and women generally. The older men tried to keep from laughing and mostly succeeded. This young man needed them.

They could sense he was becoming less tense and seemed to enjoy the father/grandfather counseling session. Their responsible love for him pervaded the whole time together.

All such teenage fellows should have this type of productive outing. Boy, did he learn a lot that day. In fact, so did they and were confidently overjoyed they could be of help.

By the time Mom figured most of this out, the threesome had built the type of generational solidarity not often witnessed in our day and time. In a way, it all seemed so simple.

Now Mom knew why the fishing was wonderful. It didn't have much to do with fishing. What had gone on was much more significant than catching the biggest catfish on record.

Sons and daughters need this kind of healthy camaraderie. It has a way of gluing us together, focusing on matters that really count. More than likely, this also influenced how the lad would treat women.

It was a moment less than one day long and it would influence a man positively the rest of his life. Mother and Grandmother could sense respect for them and other women would be a priority.

"**G**et off your cell phone," the new retiree snorted. He just despised those darn things, especially in traffic. There he sat and dozens of cars were locked into no movement.

Then, a lane—not his—would move. Each time he saw someone using a cell phone he would let it be known that was not a place to use one. They were okay, but not in a car.

Would he ever be able to make his right turn? Somehow this must be the fault of those in their cars who were glued to that thing. It was disgraceful and dangerous.

After he had told off about six or seven drivers with that thing in their ears, he began to notice something. Most every car had moved—except his. Well, that shook him up more than a little.

Finally, he heard this tapping on his window. He rolled it down and there stood a gracious young woman.

She asked him if he had car trouble and he quickly informed her he didn't.

With a touch of sarcasm, she proceeded to inform him he had sat through three green lights.

His face was red and showed signs of deep embarrassment. Surely she must be wrong about that.

The truth came out. He had been so busy telling everyone to get off their cell phones, he forgot to look at the traffic light. Drivers simply drove around him and went on their way.

It dawned on him that his need to regulate the use of those phones could have caused a major accident. To be newly retired and have that happen would be a tragic way to start a new life.

So, he sat in the local Bob Evans restaurant and became quite philosophical. Who was he to tell others to get off those things? He felt a twinge of shame.

His motivation really was quite noble. He didn't want someone injured because of poor concentration. Yet, he acknowledged to himself he was the one who lost focus.

Now, I don't know your feelings towards those little gadgets made for communication. I don't own one and rarely use one. That is not to be interpreted as a suggestion.

The reality is we are our own best law enforcement. If you think driving on the interstate in heavy traffic is a place to have a long visit with your grandmother, maybe you should think again.

If you are on your way to Chicago and the boss calls to give special instructions, maybe you should tell him or her you will call right back at the next truck stop. A little common sense goes a long way.

95 Our Self-Esteem Should Not Be Linked to What Others Think

"**I** wish I had not gone," she intoned with some melancholy. She was referring to her high school class reunion. It turned out to be not only unpleasant but quite awkward.

Twenty-five years had gone by. Her classmates came in large numbers. In fact, 78 out of 130 were present and all came in a festive mood that reflected lost memories emerging.

At their tables most everyone was comparing notes about this and that. It became evident that it was very important to some people to assess who was successful and who was not.

What began with joy really ended with mixed feelings of jealously, anger, and a bit of appreciation. As they began leaving, the mood really had changed. She felt put-down and depressed.

She thought she and her husband had done quite well in rearing a family of four children. He worked full time and she part time. She gave priority to her husband and wonderful children.

Their marriage had been solid and they never allowed differences of opinion to become ugly. Other men and women, though friends, were never allowed to penetrate their privacy.

To her surprise, several at the gathering spoke of their marriages and divorces and often remarriages in ways she thought totally unnecessary. It was as though they rather relished the experience.

She and her husband were not wealthy, but their income had provided a pleasant living with some extras. It seemed others at her table needed to talk about their stocks and bonds, owned and wished for.

Their whole family was religious, even though they were in different denominations. Some of her classmates wondered why they took religion seriously. Others found the lifestyle humorous.

She had so looked forward to the event and now most everything had gone downhill. Her husband sensed her great disappointment. It wasn't the end of the world, just disheartening.

There didn't seem to be any reason to attend the next one at the thirty-year point. Why go and be made to feel uncomfortable? Why bother with those who you once shared life but who changed so much?

Does that sound like something you have experienced? Were you going along happily and satisfied with your life until others strongly implied you didn't have a handle on modern living? Patience.

Our contributions to Christ, His Church, and our loved ones are found in keeping basic moral and religious codes. We are never bound to please anyone, except God. Go to your next reunion.

96   A Haven of Rest Found in the Church of God

"**N**othing but the blood of Jesus," kept running through his mind. He wasn't sure why. After all, he was just a boy when they sang that in the little Protestant church he attended.

Then, he began to reflect on how that small congregation, including his parents, sang it with deep feeling and a sense of saving power. Those days were long, long ago.

Since that time, his life had become painful and very complicated. He was in his early forties and his life was the proverbial "mess." Thirty years ago was the last time he was in any church.

In his sorrow and depression, it seemed like there was no way to go on. For the moment, the only ray of hope was "Nothing but the blood of Jesus" and memories of simple, happy days.

Jobs would come and go. Marriages and divorces were more than he wanted to discuss. Friends were in short supply, and frankly he couldn't count on anyone that he currently knew.

Yes, drugs and alcohol also were part of his lifestyle. They kept him drained of all the money he could borrow, beg, or steal. His plight was very sad and the end seemed near.

So, he began to wander the streets and alleys. Was there someone someplace who could help him? His sorrow only deepened, as he recalled his boyhood days of happiness.

He saw buildings he thought were churches but it had been so long since he had been in one, he wasn't quite sure. Mostly prosperous and busy people went on their ways.

Days of the week were lost and the calendar meant nothing at this stage of his life except a premature death. He slept in doorways, shelters, and dangerous alleys.

One morning, which happened to be Sunday, "Nothing but the blood of Jesus" refused to go away. He wept until there were no more tears. A pleasant surprise, however, awaited him.

People were gathering at a church and he decided to go inside. The ushers were kind and offered him a seat near the back. It had been so long he didn't know what to expect.

The man up front was clothed in white that looked like a robe. He remembered his preacher long ago being in a suit, shirt, and tie. But in the white garment he saw the purity long forgotten.

The fellow leading the service said over and over how important the blood of Jesus was. People kept coming and going to the front. He had been to Saint Mary's that day and found a new lease on life.

97   Humility and Persistence
Pay Off Once Again

"It's no use," he whimpered and whined. He had received his tenth rejection slip from a publisher. He thought he had written a best-seller and, that at least, one big publisher would agree with him.

The first three or four rejections didn't bother him much. When the tenth one came, it seemed like everything was over and no one would get the chance to read his masterpiece. He even shed tears.

So, he boxed the manuscript up and put it in the back of his closet. That was that and there was no need to pursue the matter. It was time to move on to bigger and better things.

All that seemed simple enough, except he kept sulking about the matter and feeling sorry for himself. It bothered him so much the quality of his teaching at the local high school was suffering.

Could he bear to get that thing out and send it to another publisher? He prayed about it and wasn't sure that helped much. At any rate, off went the manuscript to yet another publisher.

This time his cover letter was less formal and demanding. Yes, even one could sense a bit of humility in it. It was a different approach he didn't like very well, but maybe it would work.

After weeks of waiting, plus sending two or three reminders, he received a reply. He didn't get a form letter. While his great novel had been returned, a skilled editor had carefully read portions of it.

Much to his surprise, he was asked to write a short story and sent it. Guidelines were provided and a new lease on a possible literary career was at hand. His whining stopped.

He poured his life's blood, plus all the literary expertise he had into it. In three weeks it was in the mail. After several days a reply came, along with his short story.

The editor had used a generous amount of red marks and told him to do most of it over. How could they do that to him? He had submitted a carefully prepared and polished piece.

Fortunately, he did the rewriting and returned it with a letter of appreciation for the opportunity to be published. Now, he would soon see his name in print and his students would be admiring.

Well, it was returned again with red marks but not as many. He was not only hurt, he was ready to tell them off. He didn't and meekly did what was asked of him and waited.

In a few days a letter came, saying his work had been accepted for publication. It would be in an anthology for promising writers. There would be no payment—that hurt. But he was on his way.

98 A Faithful God Tests His Children to Help Them Grow

"Lord, it just isn't fair," the pastor cried out in his prayers. It was an age-old problem among clergy. A brother was moving ahead of him in the competition.

The pastor was dumbfounded that Brother Jones had gone to a bigger church and gotten a bigger salary. He was telling the Lord that should not be, and how about some justice?

Hadn't he been faithful to his call? Hadn't he worked hard and sacrificed at different points and times? Now, this unworthy fellow had gone around him and was gloating.

Well, dear people, in the world of clergy politics one can discover some disconcerting things. Among them are jealousies that rival and may surpass the secular world. Shame on us.

Brother Jones had not been in the ministry as long, had less education, and was certainly not as good a preacher. He didn't deserve his new big congregation and salary, that was for sure.

I am sure the Lord heard his prayer calling for fairness. Exactly what the Lord said in return, I don't know. It may have been to remind him he had been called and nothing else mattered.

You may quickly recognize the similarity between him and the elder brother in the story of the prodigal son. Why reward a son who had been out frittering away his inheritance?

You recall the older brother wondered why there was to be a celebration for someone who was a real dumb-dumb. After all, he squandered his life and should be punished or defrocked.

Isn't it interesting how we don't have a clue about God's will and try to apply our own justice? May He be merciful to us pastors who forget some of the basics of Christian living.

God is always faithful and sometimes gives us situations to make us grow. On one occasion, He pointed out I could learn something in one day or it could take ten years. Regardless, I was going to learn.

To be in the hands of a just and loving God is always to be in the right place at the right time. To be genuinely called into the ordained ministry doesn't guarantee statistical success.

In fact, downward mobility in the eyes of the world may be upward mobility in terms of spiritual growth. Standing ovations may get you most every place, except where God wants you to go.

If a pastor has a congregation who loves him and will work with him, what else is needed? I have never known a healthy church dedicated to Christ betray their obligations to their pastor.

"**I**t's too cold here," he lamented. He was half serious and half humorous. Indiana weather had gotten to him and he was not going to put up with the frigid temperatures.

He liked to poke good-natured fun at the Hoosier state, and one got the idea no one was going to keep him out of Florida for four months. There it was warm, much warmer, and no snow.

This has been a common pattern for many people for several years. We are surprised oftentimes by those who finally give in and announce they have had enough. Off they go.

It is common knowledge a large number of churches in Florida are packed during the winter months. Some of my parishioners over the years used to get about half angry at the snowbirds.

I always hated to see some really fine church members head south and be absent for months at a time. However, I began to learn something very significant. All is not lost.

Most that I knew did not become inactive or spend Sunday mornings sunning themselves on the beach or elsewhere. They were regular worshippers. In fact, some became chairpersons of projects.

Yes, and something else needs to be said. I have never known any of them to cease giving financially to their churches in Indiana. They are physically absent but the checks keep coming.

So, friends let us not begrudge those who have perhaps a bit more money than you and me. God goes with them, stays with them in the South, and comes home with them.

Isn't it delightful when they do return in late spring? My common response is to ask them to please sign the guest register, chuckle, and give them a big hug.

In all honesty, I doubt that journey to Florida or Arizona or some other warm climate will ever be my winter abode. To be honest, too many things might happen in Indiana that I don't know about.

You might respond, "Don't be too sure about that. Remember the cold unpredictable weather in our state." Ah, but what about walking in freezing weather and then going to Bob Evans for hot coffee?

Some of my best mornings are spent walking in cold weather for about an hour, praying for about the same amount of time, and then heading for my favorite restaurant. Friends, that's hard to beat.

So, if you must head south, God bless you. While you are enjoying the warmth and basking on the beach, I will be thanking God for the Indiana cold, prayer time, and Bob Evans. No envy here.

About the Author

Donald Charles Lacy was born and raised in Indiana. He served in the U.S. Navy and taught social studies and English prior to entering the ministry. Since then, he's served as a United Methodist minister for more than forty years, pastoring churches across the state, including Indianapolis. He is a nationally known leader in the field of Christian Unity, and is the author of more than a thousand published pieces. His *Collected Works* was published by Providence House Publishers in 2001.

He earned a bachelor of science degree and a master of arts degree from Ball State University, as well as a master's of divinity and a doctor of ministry degree from Christian Theological Seminary.

Over the years, he's been a member of Phi Delta Kappa, Pi Gamma Mu, Rotary, Kiwanis, Lions, Scottish Rite (Indianapolis), York Rite College (Fort Wayne), and Columbia Club (Indianapolis), among others. He and his wife, Dorothy, have four daughters: Anne Marie, Donna Jean, Sharon Elizabeth, and Martha Elaine, as well as one grandson, Fillip.